GODDESS WORSHIP, WITCHCRAFT AND NEO-PAGANISM

D0368339

Zondervan
Guide to Cults &
Religious Movements

GODDESS WORSHIP, WITCHCRAFT AND NEO-PAGANISM

CRAIG S. HAWKINS

Author

Alan W. Gomes
Series Editor

ZondervanPublishingHouse
Grand Rapids, Michigan

A Division of HarperCollins*Publishers*

Goddess Worship, Witchcraft and Neo-Paganism
Copyright © 1998 by Craig S. Hawkins

Requests for information should be addressed to:
Zondervan Publishing House
Grand Rapids, Michigan 49530

Library of Congress Cataloging-in-Publication Data

Hawkins, Craig S., 1958–
    Goddess worship, witchcraft and neo-paganism / Craig S. Hawkins.
        p.   cm. — (Zondervan guide to cults & religious movements)
    Includes bibliographical references.
    ISBN: 0-310-48881-8 (pbk.)
    1. Goddess religion—Controversial literature.   2. Neopaganism—
Controversial literature.   3. Witchcraft.   4. Apologetics   5. Evangelicalism.
    I. Title.   II. Series.
    BL473.5.H38   1998
    261.2'9—dc21   97-28257
                                                                                    CIP

Interior design by Art Jacobs

Printed in the United States of America

98 99 00 01 02 /❖ DP/ 10 9 8 7 6 5 4 3 2 1

 Contents

How to Use This Book

The *Zondervan Guide to Cults and Religious Movements* comprises fifteen volumes, treating many of the most important groups and belief systems confronting the Christian church today. This series distills the most important facts about each and presents a well-reasoned, cogent Christian response. The authors in this series are highly qualified, well-respected professional Christian apologists with considerable expertise on their topics.

We have designed the structure and layout to help you find the information you need as quickly as possible. All the volumes are written in outline form, which allows us to pack substantial content into a short book. With some exceptions, each book contains, first, an introduction to the cult, movement, or belief system. The introduction gives a brief history of the group, its organizational structure, and vital statistics such as membership. Second, the theology section is arranged by doctrinal topic, such as God, Christ, sin, and salvation. The movement's position is set forth objectively, primarily from its own official writings. The group's teachings are then refuted point by point, followed by an affirmative presentation of what the Bible says about the doctrine. The third section is a discussion of witnessing tips. While each witnessing encounter must be handled individually and sensitively, this section provides some helpful general guidelines, including both dos and don'ts. The fourth section contains annotated bibliographies, listing works by the groups themselves and books written by Christians in response. Fifth, each book has a parallel comparison chart, with direct quotations from the group's literature in the left column and the biblical refutation on the right. Some of the books conclude with a glossary.

One potential problem with a detailed outline is that it is easy to lose one's place in the overall structure. Therefore, we have provided graphical "signposts" at the top of the odd-numbered pages. Functioning like a "you are here" map in a shopping mall, these graphics show your place in the outline, including the sections that come before and after your current position. (Those familiar with modern computer software will note immediately the resemblance to a "drop-down" menu bar, where the second-level choices vary depending on the currently selected main menu item.) In the theology section we have also used "icons" in the margins to make clear at a glance whether the material is being presented from the group's viewpoint or the Christian viewpoint. For example, in the Mormonism volume the sections presenting the Mormon position are indicated with a picture resembling the angel Moroni in the margin; the biblical view is shown by a drawing of the Bible.

We hope you will find these books useful as you seek "to give an answer to everyone who asks you to give the reason for the hope that you have" (1 Peter 3:15).

— Alan W. Gomes, Ph.D.
Series Editor

# Part I: *Introduction*

I. What Is Contemporary Witchcraft?

A. *Witchcraft: One Type of Occultism*
1. Witchcraft is one specific form of occultism.
2. Witchcraft is a particular religion—a religiomagical viewpoint—within the broader context of occultism, the kingdom of the occult
3. Witchcraft is a form of neo-paganism.
   a. Most witchcraft today is part of the contemporary neo-pagan movement, which is part of the occult.
   b. Neo-paganism is the revival of the old gods and goddesses of pre-Christian polytheistic mythologies, mystery cults, and nature religions, such as Celtic, Greek, Egyptian, Roman, and Sumerian.
   c. Prudence Jones and Caitlín Matthews write: "'Pagans' are people who follow the Old Religion, the native religious tradition of Europe which predated more abstract world religions such as Christianity. . . . in a sense the new Pagans are neo-Pagans, since they derive their impetus from a spiritual re-emergence and restatement of ancient Pagan principles."[1]
   d. Neo-paganism also includes existing tribal religions, Native American religions, and shamanism.
   e. It also includes new religions inspired by avant-garde science fiction and fantasy works (e.g., the Church of All Worlds) as well as diverse occultic sources and traditions.
4. Related to witchcraft covens are other neo-pagan groups.[2]
   a. While Gardnerian witchcraft gave rise to most of the neo-pagan movement, witchcraft is now only one type of neo-paganism.[3]
   b. Other neo-pagans primarily differ from witches in their rejection of the designation *witch*.
   c. Some vary in the emphasis they place on the Goddess.
   d. Some use terms such as *nest* or *grove* rather than *coven*.

---

[1]Prudence Jones and Caitlín Matthews, eds., *Voices from the Circle: The Heritage of Western Paganism* (Wellingborough, England: Aquarian Press, 1990), 13–14.
[2]The specifics of these points are discussed later in the book.
[3]On the importance of Gardner to the modern witchcraft movement, see point V.A below.

   e. Many identify with a pre-Christian tradition, such as Celtic (Druidic), Egyptian, Greek, Native American, Norse, or Roman rather than Wiccan.

   f. Some identify with modern motifs, for example, from science fiction or avant-garde literature.

B. Diversity Within the Witchcraft (Neo-Pagan) Movement

1. The contemporary witchcraft (the entire neo-pagan) movement is very diverse and decentralized. Diversity is a hallmark.

2. Although there are respected teachers and spokespersons and more or less popular witchcraft publications within contemporary witchcraft and the broader neo-pagan movement, there is no one centralized authority for "orthodox" beliefs and practices.[4] Neo-pagans do not all subscribe to precisely the same views, beliefs, and practices.

3. The idea of uniform or standardized beliefs and practices established and enforced by some authority is not only nonexistent in contemporary witchcraft, it is despised in principle.

4. Most witches evidence a contempt for having their beliefs and practices classified.

5. The words *witch* and *witchcraft* have multiple meanings due to the ways they have been applied both today and in the past.

6. Witches disagree about what constitutes a witch or practitioner of witchcraft.[5]

C. Unity Among Diversity Within the Witchcraft Movement

1. Despite the diversity, there is, nonetheless, a core of common characteristics and beliefs in witchcraft and in the larger neo-pagan movement—that is, there are significant commonalities of beliefs and practices among contemporary neo-pagans.

2. The beliefs and practices most neo-pagans hold in common are treated in the points below.

II. Core Beliefs in Contemporary Witchcraft and Other Forms of Neo-Paganism

A. Antiauthoritarianism[6]

1. Most neo-pagans reject any type of centralized authority. Autonomy is a vital aspect of their religion.

---

[4]See Margot Adler, *Drawing Down the Moon: Witches, Druids, Goddess-Worshippers, and Other Pagans in America Today*, rev. and exp. ed. (Boston: Beacon Press, 1986), 3, 99, 100, 107, 113.

[5]See ibid., 41–43, 66–72, 99–107.

[6]See ibid., viii–ix, xii, 3, 99.

2. Aidan Kelly, a leader in the neo-pagan movement, aptly writes, "They ... are extremely anti-authoritarian, and are contemptuous of all rules and generalizations."[7]

B. *Antidogmatism*

1. Most neo-pagans disdain doctrine and theology as detrimental to the essence of religion.

2. For example, Kelly asserts, "The Craft is generally extremely anti-dogmatic in its approach. Although Witches do believe many things, belief is not a requirement for membership or initiation."[8]

3. We should not assume that most neo-pagans have carefully thought through their views. It would be a mistake to assume that most neo-pagans have systematized their beliefs (doctrines).

4. The neo-pagans' disparagement of doctrine is related to their emphasis on personal experience as the touchstone of truth.[9]

C. *Eclecticism*

1. The neo-pagan movement is very eclectic.

2. Neo-pagans freely borrow, mix and match, and synthesize views and practices from various sources to "customize" or arrive at a religion literally of their own making.

3. For example, neo-pagans borrow from ceremonial magic, grimoires,[10] psychology, philosophy, shamanism, and others.

D. *Experience*

1. Witchcraft and other forms of neo-paganism are primarily based on personal experience. Kelly writes: "What really defines a Witch is a type of *experience* people go through. These experiences depend on altered states of consciousness. The Craft is really the Yoga of the West."[11]

2. Mysticism is an important type of experience for most neo-pagans.

   a. Mysticism is in part defined as the ineffable experience of being one with all of reality or one with the divine.

   b. This mystical experience is frequently spoken of as "that feeling of ineffable oneness with all Life."[12]

---

[7] Aidan Kelly, ed., J. Gordon Melton, gen. ed., *Cults and New Religions: Neo-Pagan Witchcraft I* (New York: Garland, 1990), introduction.

[8] Aidan A. Kelly, *Crafting the Art of Magic, Book I: A History of Modern Witchcraft, 1939–1964* (St. Paul: Llewellyn, 1991), 5. See also Adler, xii.

[9] See, e.g., Adler, x, xii, 20, 27–36, 169–73, 441–42; Marian Green, *A Witch Alone* (London: Aquarian Press, 1991), 18–19; Jones and Matthews, Introduction, *Voices from the Circle*, 32, 34; T. M. Luhrmann, *Persuasions of the Witch's Craft: Ritual Magic in Contemporary England* (Cambridge: Harvard University Press, 1989), 7, 341–42; Starhawk (Miriam Simos), *The Spiral Dance: A Rebirth of the Ancient Religion of the Great Goddess* (San Francisco: Harper & Row, 1979), 2, 7–9, 77.

[10] See the glossary, Part VI.

[11] Quoted in Adler, *Drawing Down the Moon*, 106, emphasis in original.

[12] *The Covenant of the Goddess* (hereafter *COG*) information packet, Northern California Local Council Media Committee, n.d., "Basic Philosophy."

3. Neo-pagans generally have an existential view of truth.

   a. Many regard experience as superior to intellect in discovering truth.[13] One "knows" not by reason or the intellect, but by personal experience, feelings, or intuition.

   b. For many neo-pagans, truth is subjective.

   c. Ultimate or religious truth(s) are not found from an external source or revelation, such as the Bible, but from experience(s).[14]

4. Personal experience is more important than what one believes.[15]

   a. For instance, the witch Margot Adler asserts, *"Belief* has never seemed very relevant to the experiences and processes of the groups that call themselves, collectively, the Neo-Pagan movement."[16]

   b. In literature from the Covenant of the Goddess we read, "Our religion is not a series of precepts or beliefs, rather we believe that we each have within ourselves the capacity to reach out and experience the mystery—that feeling of ineffable oneness with all Life."[17]

5. What one does (practices) is more important than what one believes.

   a. Neo-pagans define themselves more by what they do or experience than by what they believe.

   b. For example, Adler, referring to remarks by Kelly, comments, "The Craft, unlike Christianity and other world religions, is totally defined in terms of the ritual—of what people *do*—and not what people *believe.*"[18]

E. *Ethics*

1. The "Wiccan Rede" or "Pagan Ethic"

   a. The primary ethical principle of neo-pagans is the "Pagan Ethic," or "Wiccan Rede." (*Rede* is an archaic term for counsel or advice.)

   b. One version of the Rede states, "If it [or you] harm none, do what you will [want]."

   c. Another version of this rule—referred to as the "Pagan Ethic"— states, "Do what thou will, but harm none."

---

[13]See, e.g., Laurie Cabot and Tom Cowan, *Power of the Witch* (New York: Dell, 1989), 146; Stewart Farrar, *What Witches Do: The Modern Coven Revealed* (London: Sphere Books, 1973), 198; Luhrmann, *Persuasions,* 256–57; Starhawk, *Spiral Dance,* 9, 77; Marion Weinstein, *Positive Magic: Occult Self-Help,* rev. ed. (Custer, Wash.: Phoenix, 1981), 10–11, 14.

[14]See, e.g., Adler, *Drawing Down the Moon,* 166, 170–71, 442; Luhrmann, *Persuasions,* 253–54, 257, 325; Janet Farrar and Stewart Farrar, *A Witches Bible Compleat* (New York: Magickal Childe, 1991), 1:30; Starhawk, *Spiral Dance,* 7–9, 77, 84.

[15]See, e.g., Adler, *Drawing Down the Moon,* x.

[16]Ibid., 20, emphasis in original; see also Green, *A Witch Alone,* 18–19.

[17]*COG* information packet, "Basic Philosophy."

[18]Adler, *Drawing Down the Moon,* 170, emphasis in original; see also 20, 305, 307, 441.

2. Conscience
    a. Alex Sanders, the founder of Alexandrian witchcraft, said, "A thing is good for me until I feel it's not right for me."[19]
    b. The witch Stewart Farrar writes, "The witch's own conscience is and must be the final arbiter, and if it rebels against some suggestions from [the] High Priest, High Priestess, or anyone else, he must follow his conscience."[20]
3. Love for Life
    a. Janet and Stewart Farrar say, "Love and respect for Mother Earth and all her creatures" is a vital aspect of witches' ethics.[21]
    b. Starhawk (Miriam Simos) says: "In spite of diversity, there are ethics and values that are common to all traditions of Witchcraft. They are based on the concept of the Goddess as immanent in the world and in all forms of life, including human beings.... Love for life in all its forms is the basic ethic of Witchcraft."[22]
4. Ethical Relativism
    a. Vivianne Crowley, a high priestess, writes, "In the circle there are no absolutes; no rights and wrongs."[23]
    b. The witch Doreen Valiente, "... the witches have a saying: 'The circle of the coven is between the worlds and what takes place between the worlds is no concern of either world' (or as some versions give it, 'no concern of this world')."[24]
5. Other miscellaneous ethical guidelines include common sense, the general consensus of the witchcraft or neo-pagan community, the laws of the state, pragmatic considerations, science, and others.

F. *Open Metaphysic*
1. Many neo-pagans hold to the concept of an "open metaphysic."[25] It is called different names among neo-pagans but is substantially the same.
2. The open metaphysical concept is that "reality is multiple and diverse." That is, there are innumerable, if not infinite, levels of and meanings to reality and truth.
3. There is no single view of reality, or system of logic, that is adequate or complete to grasp or accommodate the complexity (due to the incredible multiplicity) of reality and truth.

---

[19]Farrar, *What Witches Do*, 49.

[20]Ibid., 52. See also Sybil Leek, *The Complete Art of Witchcraft* (New York: Signet Books, 1971), 58.

[21]Farrar and Farrar, *Witches Bible Compleat*, 2:138.

[22]Starhawk, *Spiral Dance*, 11.

[23]Vivianne Crowley, "The Initiation," in Jones and Matthews, *Voices from the Circle*, 82.

[24]Doreen Valiente, *Witchcraft for Tomorrow* (Custer, Wash.: Phoenix, 1987), 148.

[25]See, e.g., Adler, *Drawing Down the Moon*, 25, 29, 36, 38, 169, 172; Philip Emmons Isaac Bonewits, *Real Magic*, rev. ed. (York Beach, Maine: Samuel Weiser, 1989), 11–14; Cabot and Cowan, *Power of the*

4. Thus, no one person or religious or philosophical perspective definitively comprehends ultimate reality.

   a. No one person or perspective has the corner on truth or can assert that his or her views are the only correct ones.

   b. We should not limit ourselves to one narrow perspective or religion.

   c. We should be open-minded and tolerant and should embrace diverse viewpoints. (See next point.)

G. *Tolerance*

1. Tolerance is a highly touted trait among neo-pagans.

2. Tolerance of all "life-affirming" ideologies, philosophies, and religions is viewed as virtuous and a sign of maturity.

3. Diversity of beliefs and practices is seen as healthy and as necessary for the survival and harmony of humanity and the planet.

4. "Intolerance" of the viability or validity of other religious perspectives is viewed as "religious imperialism."

5. Tenet ten of the Council of American Witches'[26] "Principles of Wiccan Belief," adopted in 1974, states, "Our only animosity toward Christianity, or toward any other religion or philosophy-of-life, is to the extent that its institutions have claimed to be 'the only way' and have sought to deny freedom to others and to suppress other ways of religious practice and belief."[27]

6. Witches Arnold and Patricia Crowther write: "They [witches] are very tolerant of all religions and think that each person should be allowed to choose his own god and way of worship. They do not understand why other religions should wish to convert everyone to their own way of thinking."[28]

H. *Animism*

1. Many neo-pagans are animists.

2. As used by neo-pagans, animism is the view that the "Life Force" is immanent within all of creation. All is infused with and participates in the vital Life Force, or energy.

3. Thus, the entire earth is a living organism. In some significant sense, all of nature is alive. All of nature is animate.

4. Janet and Stewart Farrar write, "Witches are dedicated to the concept of the Earth as a living organism. And this attitude—physical,

---

Witch, 153–54, 180, 300; Farrar and Farrar, *Witches Bible Compleat,* 2:106–7, 109, 113; Luhrmann, *Persuasions,* 292, 342; Weinstein, *Positive Magic,* 25–26, 27.

[26]This group is now defunct.

[27]The full list of principles can be found in Adler, *Drawing Down the Moon,* 101–3.

[28]Arnold Crowther and Patricia Crowther, *The Secrets of Ancient Witchcraft with the Witches Tarot* (Secaucus, N.J.: Citadel Press, 1974), 159.

mental, psychic, and spiritual—is the heart and soul of the Old Religion."[29]

I. Hylozoism

1. Some neo-pagans are hylozoists.[30]
2. Hylozoism is the idea that everything, even "inanimate" matter, is in some literal sense alive or intrinsically active and responsive.
3. Thus, even a rock is active—that is, not inert or passive.

J. Panpsychism[31]

1. Some neo-pagans are panpsychists.[32]
2. Panpsychism is similar but not identical to animism and hylozoism.[33]
3. Panpsychism is the view that all objects in the universe have an "inner," or psychological, being. Thus, everything possesses or has some level of consciousness
4. Some panpsychists postulate that every object has a mind, soul, or spirit. If a witch or other neo-pagan also holds that mind, soul, or spirit entails life, then that person would also be a hylozoist.[34]
5. Some neo-pagans believe, either literally or metaphorically, that all matter (even plants and "inanimate" objects) have some type of awareness or consciousness.
   a. Thus, all of reality is a continuum of consciousness.
   b. Laurie Cabot, the "official witch of Salem," comments, "Each plant, animal, rock, river, hill, path, shadow, fire, or twig has its own spirit, its own intelligence, a message."[35]
   c. The witch Marion Weinstein writes: "Crystals are alive. . . . Spend time with each crystal and allow it to reveal to you what its purpose is in your life. You may find that it actually speaks to you. The messages may be as clear as those of a spirit voice."[36]

---

[29]Farrar and Farrar, *Witches Bible Compleat*, 2:136–37.

[30]Correspondence with Paul Suliin, the Deputy National Coordinator of the Pagan/Occult/Witchcraft Special Interest Group (POWSIG) of Mensa. See Starhawk, *Spiral Dance*, 29.

[31]The distinctions among animism, hylozoism, and panpsychism are subtle. Nonetheless, for the sake of accuracy, such distinctions should be made.

[32]Correspondence with Paul Suliin. See Starhawk, *Spiral Dance*, 29.

[33]For a thorough treatment of panpsychism and hylozoism, see the article "Panpsychism" by Paul Edwards in *The Encyclopedia of Philosophy*, ed. Paul Edwards, reprint ed. (New York: Macmillan and Free Press, 1972), 6:22–30.

[34]That is, having a mind, soul, or spirit entails or means that the entity is a living entity, not merely a conscious one. According to one version of this view, something can be conscious but not a living (biological) entity. A contemporary example is a computer: A computer could have a form of consciousness or artificial intelligence but not be a biologically living entity.

[35]Cabot and Cowan, *Power of the Witch*, 302.

[36]Marion Weinstein, *Earth Magic: A Dianic Book of Shadows*, rev. and exp. ed. (Custer, Wash.: Phoenix, 1980, 1986), 18.

K. Nature-Oriented Religious Movement

1. Many neo-pagans worship nature.

2. It is not so much that they worship objects of nature per se—though some do—but the creative Life Force or power, especially as manifested in nature.

3. Others do not worship nature but have a very high regard for it.

4. They seek to live in harmony and be physically in tune with nature.

5. Neo-pagan religions see themselves as life-affirming religions.

6. The earth is a (or the) manifestation of the Goddess and God. All is seen as sacred; all is to be revered.

L. Polytheism

1. Many neo-pagans are polytheists.[37] (As will be seen, many neo-pagans are generally polytheists and/or pantheists and/or panentheists.)

2. As defined by neo-pagans, polytheism is not only the belief in and/or worship of diverse deities, but also the belief in multiple levels of and meanings to reality—the open metaphysic already referenced.[38]

3. In allowing for the existence of multiple deities, it also allows a multiplicity of religions and views of reality—some mutually exclusive.

4. Thus, neo-pagans can ally themselves with a certain goddess and/or god, or group thereof, but still grant the viability of other religions and perspectives.[39] This perspective manifests itself in the view that there is no one way or right religion for all, or no "one truth."

5. In light of their polytheistic perspective, many neo-pagans may believe in and/or invoke a pantheon of goddesses and gods besides the Mother Goddess and Horned God, which are the two primary deities for many neo-pagans (see points II.R and II.S).

6. Some neo-pagans believe in good and evil extradimensional or intermediate beings or entities, including so-called higher and lower life forms (relative to humans), such as angels or demons, elemental spirits, extraterrestrial entities, spirit guides/guardians, and teachers.

7. Neo-pagans hold various views as to the nature of these creatures.

   a. Some see them as mere metaphors, myths, or symbols.

   b. Others see them as manifestations of the One (see II.P and II.Q), or as literal individual entities in their own right.[40]

---

[37]This will be discussed in greater detail in Part II, Section III.

[38]See point II.F. above.

[39]See Part II, Section III.B.1.

[40]See, e.g., Raymond Buckland, *Buckland's Complete Book of Witchcraft* (St. Paul: Llewellyn, 1988), 155; Cabot and Cowan, *Power of the Witch,* 153, 197–98, 203, 276, 283–84, 300–301; Crowther and Crowther, *Secrets of Ancient Witchcraft,* 75, 88, 153–54, 200–202; Farrar, *What Witches Do,* 45, 56, 81–84, 143–45, 159–67; Farrar and Farrar, *Witches Bible Compleat,* 2:83, 119, 123, 139; Gavin Frost and Yvonne Frost, *The Magic Power of Witchcraft* (West Nyack, N.Y.: Parker, 1976), 140–41, 145, 192–93; Amber K., "Beginning True Magick," in Kelly, *Neo-Pagan Witchcraft I,* 290; Leek, *Complete Art of Witchcraft,* 25–26, 44–45, 155; Gregg Stafford,

8. As for demons and other evil entities, some neo-pagans deny their existence, while others believe they exist.[41]

M. Pantheism

1. Many neo-pagans are pantheists.[42]

2. Pantheism is the view that all is god or divine. All is god and god is all. There is a one-to-one correspondence between divinity and creation.

N. Panentheism

1. Many neo-pagans are panentheists.[43]

2. Panentheism is the view that the world is a manifestation of, or is contained in, the divine. While the divine is immanent in the world, it still transcends the universe to some degree.

3. As the human body is to the mind or soul, analogously, the universe is to the divine

4. All that exists is part of and imbued with divinity yet it is not the totality of the Divinity.

O. Divinity As Immanent in Nature and Humanity

1. In light of the previous two views, many neo-pagans view divinity as immanent in and inseparable from nature and humanity.[44]

2. Hence, all of nature is divine.

3. Therefore, humans are divine (or potentially so).

4. Thus, all life and all life-forms are held as sacred by neo-pagans.

P. Monism

1. Many neo-pagans are monists.[45]

"The Medicine Circle of Turtle Island," in Jones and Matthews, *Voices from the Circle,* 84, 86–89; Susan Roberts, *Witches, U.S.A.* (New York: Dell, 1971), prologue, 24, 71–75, 171–78, 189–94; Kaledon Naddair, "Pictish and Keltic Shamanism," in Jones and Matthews, *Voices from the Circle,* 94, 99–103; Starhawk, *Truth or Dare: Encounters with Power, Authority, and Magic* (San Francisco: Harper & Row, 1987), 25, 104; Doreen Valiente, *An ABC of Witchcraft: Past and Present* (New York: St. Martin's Press, 1973), 14; Doreen Valiente, *Natural Magic* (Custer, Wash.: Phoenix, 1991), 163; Weinstein, *Earth Magic,* 46–48, 56; Weinstein, *Positive Magic,* 30–31, 122.

[41]See, e.g., Adler, *Drawing Down the Moon,* 109, 159; Bonewits, *Real Magic,* 41–42; Buckland, *Complete Book of Witchcraft,* 155; Crowther and Crowther, *Secrets of Ancient Witchcraft,* 75, 153; Farrar, *What Witches Do,* 24, 81, 103; Farrar and Farrar, *Witches Bible Compleat,* 2:47, 83, 85, 119, 139; Frost and Frost, *Magic Power,* 18, 127, 132–33, 145; Justine Glass, *Witchcraft, the Sixth Sense* (North Hollywood, Calif.: Wilshire Book Company, 1974), 79; Amber K., "Beginning True Magick," 290; Leek, *Complete Art of Witchcraft,* 72, 91; Roberts, *Witches, U.S.A.,* 171–78, 186–95; Starhawk, *Spiral Dance,* 142, 145–46, 148; Weinstein, *Earth Magic,* 46, 56; Weinstein, *Positive Magic,* 39.

[42]This will be discussed further in Part II, Section III.

[43]This will be discussed in detail in Part II, Section III.

[44]This will be discussed in detail in Part II, Section III.B.2–3.

[45]See, e.g., Adler, *Drawing Down the Moon,* 35–36, 112; Bonewits, *Real Magic,* 208–9; Cabot and Cowan, *Power of the Witch,* 13, 151–52, 161, 171, 201; Crowley, "The Initiation," 79; Scott Cunningham, *The Truth About Witchcraft Today* (St. Paul: Llewellyn, 1988), 19–20; Farrar, *What Witches Do,* 40–42; Amber K., "Beginning True Magick," 288, 291; Leek, *Complete Art of Witchcraft,* 50, 56, 110, 196; Roberts, *Witches, U.S.A.,* 203; Jeffrey B. Russell, *A History of Witchcraft: Sorcerers, Heretics and Pagans* (New York: Thames and Hudson, 1982), 33, 160; Starhawk, *Dreaming the Dark: Magic, Sex and Politics,* new ed. (Boston: Beacon Press, 1988), 72; Starhawk, *Spiral Dance,* 25, 26, 195, 197; Valiente, *Witchcraft for Tomorrow,* 46, 171–72; Weinstein, *Earth Magic,* 4, 47, 92; Weinstein, *Positive Magic,* 68, 70, 72, 205, 211.

2. Monism is the view that all reality is one, or that everything can be explained in terms of one single principle, constituent, source, or substance (e.g., energy, God, mind, matter, spirit). All ultimately originates from the quintessential One.[46]

3. Paul Suliin confirms this point: "Although we are polytheists we are fundamentally monists."[47]

4. Starhawk says: "All things are one, yet each thing is separate, individual, unique. . . . The world of separate things is the reflection of the One; the One is the reflection of the myriad separate things of the world."[48]

5. For most neo-pagans the monistic "material," the "One," is the Divinity. All is one and the One is divine. All is divine.

6. Some neo-pagans, such as Aidan Kelly, would strongly disagree with the designation of "monism" for their views.[49] Nonetheless, it correctly describes the views of many, if not most, neo-pagans.

7. They see no ultimate dichotomy between matter and spirit.

Q. The Principle of Polarity

1. Polarity is a key concept for many neo-pagans.

2. The "One" is manifested in plurality—myriad forms—but primarily in polarity or duality. Thus, there is a plurality, predominately dualistic, within the One.

3. Starhawk, for instance, writes: "The view of the All as an energy field polarized by two great forces, Female and Male, Goddess and God, which in their ultimate being are aspects of each other, is common to almost all traditions of the Craft."[50]

4. The fourth tenet of "Principles of Wiccan Belief" of the Council of American Witches states in part, "We conceive of the Creative Power in the Universe as manifesting through polarity—as masculine and feminine—and that this same Creative Power lives in all people, and functions through the interaction of the masculine and feminine."

5. The Goddess and God are also dual manifestations of the monistic One. They are the primary manifestations of the monistic Divinity.[51]

R. The Mother or Triple Goddess

1. Most neo-pagans believe in, invoke, or worship the Goddess.

2. Many neo-pagans emphasize the Mother Goddess and Horned God, while witches primarily worship them.

---

[46]Peter Angeles, *Dictionary of Philosophy* (New York: Barnes & Noble, 1981), s.v. "monism."
[47]Suliin, correspondence.
[48]Starhawk, *Spiral Dance,* 25.
[49]Adler, *Drawing Down the Moon,* 34; Kelly, *Crafting the Art,* 5–6.
[50]Starhawk, *Spiral Dance,* 26.
[51]See Cunningham, *Truth About Witchcraft,* 117; Weinstein, *Positive Magic,* 68; Jones and Matthews, *Voices from the Circle,* 222.

3. Neo-pagans also diverge in the prominence they attribute to the Mother Goddess versus the Horned God. Some emphasize the Goddess, others the Horned God. Most seek a balance between the two.

4. She is seen as immanent, hence, accessible to humans.

5. As the Mother Goddess she has three primary roles: mother, maiden, and crone. Crone refers to her role, among others, as destroyer (e.g., the one who brings about death).

6. She is associated with the moon, its three phases, and the earth.

7. She is viewed as being eternal.

8. She is known and invoked under the following titles: Aphrodite, Artemis, Astaroth, Astarte, Athene, Brigit, Ceres, Cerridwen, Cybele, Diana, Demeter, Friga, Gaia, Hecate, Isis, Kali, Kore, Lilith, Luna, Nuit, Persephone, and Venus. Diana is probably the most popular.

9. Neo-pagans hold varying views concerning the identity or nature of the Goddess—a literal goddess, a simple symbol, a Jungian archetype, or a personification, to a symbol and/or emanation from or manifestation of the eternal, genderless, monistic, universal Life Force, to complete skepticism.[52]

S. The Horned God

1. Many neo-pagans also believe in, experience, invoke, and/or worship the Horned God, the Goddess's consort.

2. He is seen as immanent, hence, accessible to humans.

3. He is viewed as the lord of animals, the woods, and the hunt.

4. He is also seen as the lord of death and what lies beyond its doors. He dies and is reborn each year.

5. He is associated with the sun.

6. He is also known as, invoked as, or called Adonis, Ammon-Ra, Apollo, Cernunnos, Dionysius, Eros, Faunus, Hades, Horus, Karnayna, Osiris, Pan, Thor, and Woden. Pan seems to be the most popular.

7. Neo-pagans hold varying views regarding the Horned God. They are the same as the views held regarding the Goddess (see point R.9 above).

T. Reincarnation

1. Many neo-pagans (and certainly most witches) believe in some form of reincarnation.[53]

2. Karma is the alleged universal law of cause and effect that governs reincarnation. Every action that has moral implications has corresponding consequences, or karma, whether negative or positive or good or bad.

---

[52]For a full treatment of these varying views (six primary ones) see my book *Witchcraft: Exploring the World of Wicca* (Grand Rapids: Baker, 1996).

[53]This is discussed in greater detail in Part II, Section VIII.A–B.

U. "The Charge of the Goddess"

1. "The Charge of the Goddess," written by Gerald Gardner and Doreen Valiente in the 1950s, is the supposed traditional address of the Goddess, spoken by the high priestess to her worshipers. It conveys the essence of witchcraft or goddess worship.

2. Many neo-pagans subscribe to one form or another of "The Charge of the Goddess."[54] It is likely the most well-received statement among witches regarding the essence of contemporary witchcraft.

3. Janet and Stewart Farrar declare that this statement is "the unique and definitive statement of Wiccan philosophy."[55]

V. Magical Worldview

1. Many neo-pagans have a magical worldview. Magic/sorcery is a vital part of many neo-pagans' world and religion.

2. Working magic is the ability or the attempt to cause changes to occur in conformity with one's will—to bend, control, direct, influence, manipulate, or turn reality for one's objectives, not merely by mundane means. This is allegedly accomplished by invoking or utilizing mysterious or invisible forces, spirits, or other extradimensional entities, or relatively unknown forces, laws, powers, or rules to manipulate reality. Magic as used here means sorcery. It should not be confused with prestidigitation or sleight-of-hand.

3. There are numerous understandings among neo-pagans as to how or why magic works (see Part II, Sections V.A–B).

III. Practices of Contemporary Neo-Paganism

A. The Eight Sabbats

1. Eight primary annual holidays are celebrated in witchcraft and among other neo-pagans. They are called sabbats.

2. These seasonal celebrations are centered around the solar cycles. They are times of feasting and festivities as well as of working magic.

3. There are four greater, or major, sabbats and four lesser, or minor, ones. The four greater sabbats occur halfway between the solstices and equinoxes. The four lesser sabbats correspond to the summer and winter solstices and the spring (vernal) and autumn (fall) equinoxes.

---

[54]This is certainly true of Gardnerian, Alexandrian, and some other witches. See, e.g., Adler, *Drawing Down the Moon,* 57–58, 118; Cabot and Cowan, *Power of the Witch,* 67; Crowley, "The Initiation," 78; Farrar, *What Witches Do,* 197–98; Farrar and Farrar, *Witches Bible Compleat,* 1:15, 28, 42–43; 2:319; Rosemary Ellen Guiley, *The Encyclopedia of Witches and Witchcraft* (New York: Facts on File, 1989), s.v. "Charge of the Goddess"; Leek, *Complete Art of Witchcraft,* 189–91; Starhawk, *Spiral Dance,* 76–77, 82.

[55]Farrar and Farrar, *Witches Bible Compleat,* 1:15.

B. Esbats

1. Esbats are the regular working coven meetings of witches. Initiations and witchcraft teaching and training sessions (e.g., training in divination and magic) take place, as well as the practice or performance of rituals. General coven business is also conducted.

2. The esbats correspond to the lunar calendar, often being held on or around full or new moons or other regularly predetermined intervals.

C. Altered States of Consciousness

1. The Importance of Altered States of Consciousness

   a. Altered states of consciousness are viewed by many witches (and other neo-pagans) as a vital element of witchcraft.[56] They are used in the practice of divination, the working of magic, and spiritism.

   b. Aidan Kelly comments, *"The craft of the Craft is the craft of producing altered states of consciousness, and, traditionally, always has been."*[57]

   c. Margot Adler writes, "Those who do magic are those who work with techniques that alter consciousness in order to facilitate psychic activity."[58]

2. Trance States

   a. Trance states, one type of altered state of consciousness, are commonly practiced among neo-pagans.[59]

   b. Some neo-pagans believe that in some instances while in these trance states one can be possessed by the Goddess, the God, or some other disincarnate entity. The two most popular and common trance states among witches are termed "drawing down the moon" and "drawing down the sun."

   c. Drawing down the moon (Goddess).

      (1) In this trance state the Goddess enters or possesses a priestess or the high priestess. Some believe that they evoke the Goddess from within themselves.[60]

      (2) Often mediumistic utterances are spoken or magic worked.

      (3) For many this is the high point of rites and occultic practices.

---

[56]See Adler, *Drawing Down the Moon,* 106, 153–54, 157, 161, 165.

[57]Quoted in ibid., 153, emphasis in original.

[58]Ibid., 154.

[59]See, for example, Valiente, *An ABC of Witchcraft,* 157.

[60]See, e.g., Adler, *Drawing Down the Moon,* 19–20, 25, 109, 168; Cabot and Cowan, *Power of the Witch,* 103, 113, 115–16; Crowther and Crowther, *Secrets of Ancient Witchcraft,* 82–83; Cunningham, *Truth About Witchcraft,* 91; Gernia Dunwich, *Wicca Craft: The Modern Witch's Book of Herbs, Magick, and Dreams* (New York: Citadel Press, 1991), 58; Farrar, *What Witches Do,* 68–69, 207, 208; Farrar and Farrar, *Witches Bible Compleat,* 1:28, 40–42; 2:67–68, 168; Leek, *Complete Art of Witchcraft,* 43; Luhrmann, *Persuasions,* 50, 134.

(4) For witches, Adler asserts, "'Drawing down the moon' symbolizes the idea that we are the gods, or can, at least, become them from time to time in rite and fantasy."[61]

d. Drawing down the sun (Horned God).

(1) In this trance state the Horned God enters or possesses a priest or the high priest. Some believe that they evoke the Horned God from within themselves.

(2) Often mediumistic utterances are spoken or magic worked.

(3) As with drawing down the moon, for many witches, particularly males, this is the high point of their rites and occultic practices.

e. Channeling

Trance states are a type of what today is popularly termed "channeling." Raymond Buckland, Laurie Cabot, and Scott Cunningham all view some trances states as a type of channeling.[62]

3. Possession

a. Neo-pagans can be possessed by "various entities" by performing rituals and related practices.[63] Some neo-pagans seek possession—at least certain types and at certain times. Others seek to avoid possession completely or of certain types or in certain situations.

b. Alex Sanders was one who sought certain types of possession. Referring to one of the spirits who supposedly healed people while working through him, Sanders said: "I feel one of my spirits . . . filling my body till I'm much bigger, hiding inside me and controlling me. . . . Then I feel as though I'm being pulled up through a big hole in the back of my head, and something else is walking in."[64]

c. The witch Sharon Devlin says: "Many things are lacking in modern Paganism. For example, in all indigenous paganism possession of the participants by the gods and goddesses occurred frequently. This is not occurring frequently among Neo-Pagans and I consider it to be a sign of ill health in the Pagan movement."[65]

D. Divination

1. Divination is the attempt to obtain information regarding the past, present, or future by occultic means. Forms of divination include altered states of consciousness (e.g., channeling or other trance states),

---

[61]Adler, *Drawing Down the Moon,* 25.

[62]See Buckland, *Complete Book of Witchcraft,* 101–3, 105–6; Cabot and Cowan, *Power of the Witch,* 116; Cunningham, *Truth About Witchcraft,* 91.

[63]See, e.g., notes 59–62; Amber K., "Beginning True Magick," 290; Farrar, *What Witches Do,* 153–54; Frost and Frost, *Magic Power,* 18, 133, 137–40, 201; Sybil Leek, *Diary of a Witch* (New York: Signet Books, 1969), 151, 159–60, 203, 206; Roberts, *Witches, U.S.A.,* 24, 71–75, 174, 194–95; Starhawk, *Spiral Dance,* 142, 148.

[64]Quoted in Farrar, *What Witches Do,* 153–54.

[65]Quoted in Adler, *Drawing Down the Moon,* 142.

astrology, crystal gazing, *I Ching*, mediumship, numerology, palmistry, runes, scrying, and tarot cards among others.

2. Divination is a common practice among many neo-pagans.[66]

E. Magic/Sorcery

1. Magic/sorcery (terms used here synonymously) and other "occultic technologies"[67] are prominent in the religion of many neo-pagans.[68]

2. Scott Cunningham comments: "In Wicca it's [magic] given a more prominent place.... Wicca is a religion that embraces magic."[69]

3. Stewart Farrar remarks, "Wicca is magic."[70]

4. Janet and Stewart Farrar say, "Spell-working is a regular part of most ordinary coven Circles."[71]

5. Starhawk tells us, "Magic ... is an element common to all traditions of Witchcraft" and "Magic is the craft of Witchcraft."[72]

F. Psychic Development

1. For many neo-pagans the development of "psychic abilities" is an integral aspect of their religion.[73] Psychic development includes training for proficiency in magic, divination, spiritism, and "occultic arts and technologies" by utilizing one's purported psychic abilities.

2. Stewart Farrar writes, "The central aim of Wicca is the spiritual and psychic development of each individual witch."[74]

3. Literature from the Covenant of the Goddess states: "Most covens provide some degree of training in psychic development to strengthen

---

[66]See, e.g., Adler, *Drawing Down the Moon,* 159; Bonewits, *Real Magic,* 177–95; Buckland, *Complete Book of Witchcraft,* 111–34; Cabot and Cowan, *Power of the Witch,* 137–41, 172; Chas S. Clifton, ed., *Witchcraft Today, Book One: The Modern Craft Movement* (St. Paul: Llewellyn, 1992), 2, 14; Crowther and Crowther, *Secrets of Ancient Witchcraft,* 99–128; Cunningham, *Truth About Witchcraft,* 162–63, 168–69; Farrar and Farrar, *Witches Bible Compleat,* 2:200–211; Green, *A Witch Alone,* 113–29; Leek, *Diary,* 168–86; Starhawk, *Spiral Dance,* 36, 136, 156; Valiente, *Natural Magic,* 22–32, 115–64; Weinstein, *Positive Magic,* 80, 129–97.

[67]See, e.g., Adler, *Drawing Down the Moon,* 153–68; Bonewits, *Real Magic, passim;* Buckland, *Complete Book of Witchcraft,* 101–34, 155–74; Cabot and Cowan, *Power of the Witch,* 92–263; Farrar, *What Witches Do,* 53–177; Glass, *Sixth Sense,* 20, 94; Leek, *Diary,* 151–53, 168–86; 202–6, 211; Starhawk, *Spiral Dance,* 37, 108–58; Valiente, *Natural Magic, passim;* Weinstein, *Earth Magic,* 16–20, 27–29, 37–67; Weinstein, *Positive Magic,* 69, 129–256.

[68]This will be discussed in detail in Part II, Section V. For references to the importance of magic in witchcraft, see, e.g., Cunningham, *Truth About Witchcraft,* 62, 64–65, 158, 171; Farrar, *What Witches Do,* 65, 137, 197; Leek, *Diary,* 13; Roberts, *Witches, U.S.A.,* 23–25; Starhawk, *Spiral Dance,* 13, 109, 192; Valiente, *An ABC of Witchcraft,* 12–14, 270–73; Weinstein, *Positive Magic,* 8–10.

[69]Cunningham, *Truth About Witchcraft,* 64–65.

[70]Farrar, *What Witches Do,* 137.

[71]Farrar and Farrar, *Witches Bible Compleat,* 2:239.

[72]Starhawk, *Spiral Dance,* 13, 109.

[73]See, e.g., Bonewits, *Real Magic,* 34–35, 197, 263; Buckland, *Complete Book of Witchcraft,* 101; Cabot and Cowan, *Power of the Witch,* 172, 177, 183; COG, "General Practices," 2; Farrar, *What Witches Do,* 45–46, 63; Farrar and Farrar, *Witches Bible Compleat,* 1:12, 17–18; 2:68, 169, 279; Sybil Leek, *Reincarnation: The Second Chance* (New York: Bantam Books, 1975), 43–44, 52; Roberts, *Witches, U.S.A.,* 25; Starhawk, *Spiral Dance,* 37, 135, 144.

[74]Farrar, *What Witches Do,* 63.

21

each member's ability to participate in the religious activities. . . . We see psychic abilities as a natural human potential. We are dedicated to developing this and all of our positive human potentials."[75]

G. Spiritism

1. Many neo-pagans are involved in some form of spiritism.[76] Spiritism is contacting, interacting with, or trafficking with spirits. This includes for some neo-pagans alleged angels, demons, departed humans, extradimensional entities, spirit guides/guardians, and other noncorporeal entities.

2. Many neo-pagans practice necromancy.[77] Necromancy is one form of spiritism. It is the attempt to contact or summon the spirits of the dead.[78]

IV. Common Misconceptions Regarding Witchcraft

A. Stereotypes That Mislead

1. Most of the stereotypical images people have of contemporary witches and witchcraft do not correspond to the facts.

2. For instance, the view that witches are ugly old hags dressed in black capes and cone-shaped hats who ride broomsticks is certainly incorrect.

3. The notion that all witches are women is likewise incorrect.

4. As silly as these stereotypes are, they indicate the prevalence of misunderstandings about contemporary witches and witchcraft.

B. Witchcraft Not Just Another Name for Occultism

1. *Witchcraft* is not a generic term for all forms of occultism.

2. Thus, witchcraft is not merely the belief in or practice of astrology, crystal gazing, mediumship, Ouija boards, palm or tarot card reading, scrying, spell casting, trance states, or other forms of occultism.

3. Witchcraft is not ceremonial or ritual magic, although some witches do practice this form of occultism.

4. Millions of people believe in and/or practice some form(s) of the occult but are not witches.

---

[75]*COG,* "General Practices," 2.

[76]See, e.g., Cabot and Cowan, *Power of the Witch,* 197–98, 276, 278, 283–84; Crowther and Crowther, *Secrets of Ancient Witchcraft,* 200–202; Farrar, *What Witches Do,* 81–84, 143–44, 159–60; Frost and Frost, *Magic Power,* 140–41, 192–93, 199–200; Leek, *Complete Art of Witchcraft,* 45, 72, 155; Naddair, "Pictish and Keltic Shamanism," 99–103; Roberts, *Witches, U.S.A.,* 71–75, 174, 189–95; Stafford, "The Medicine Circle of Turtle Island," 84, 86–89; Valiente, *An ABC of Witchcraft,* 142, 152, 157; Weinstein, *Earth Magic,* 43–45, 46–48, 50, 52–54. Spiritism will be discussed in Part II, Section IX.B.4.

[77]See, e.g., Cabot and Cowan, *Power of the Witch,* 119, 121; Clifton, *Witchcraft Today,* 102; Crowther and Crowther, *Secrets of Ancient Witchcraft,* 88, 154, 200–202; Farrar and Farrar, *Witches Bible Compleat,* 1:130; 2:120; Frost and Frost, *Magic Power,* 118, 127, 129, 140–56; Leek, *Diary,* 151, 159–60, 203, 206; Beth Neilson and Imogen Cavanaugh, "She of Many Names," in Jones and Matthews, *Voices from the Circle,* 123; Valiente, *An ABC of Witchcraft,* 152, 157, 197–98; Weinstein, *Earth Magic,* 52–54.

[78]Necromancy will be discussed in detail in Part II, Section IX.B.4.

C. *Witchcraft and Other Forms of Neo-Paganism Not to Be Confused with Satanism*[79]

1. Satanism is another belief system or type of occultism.

2. Material from the Covenant of the Goddess that addresses the question of whether witches worship the devil counters: "No. Worship of Satan is a practice of profaning Christian symbolism and thus is a Christian heresy rather than a Pagan religion. The gods of the Witches are in no way connected with Satanic practice. Most Witches do not even believe Satan exists and certainly do not worship him."[80]

3. "The Pagan religions of Europe, including Druidism, Wicca and Asatru, are not derived from Christianity and have nothing to do with Satanism, which is a perversion of Christianity, but are an independent religious path, celebrating the Godhead, which all religions seek to contact, particularly in its feminine form of the Great Goddess, Mother of all things."[81]

4. Thus, neo-pagans see their religion as a viable worldview in its own right, not, like satanism, as a reaction or reversal of Christianity.

D. *Rejection of Animal or Human Sacrifices by Witches*

1. Witches, witchcraft, and other neo-pagans as discussed in this work are not involved in animal, let alone human, sacrifices.[82]

2. Due to their beliefs that all of life is sacred and that divinity permeates all creation, witches and other neo-pagans do not sacrifice animals or humans.

V. Historical Background of Modern Goddess Worship, Witchcraft, and Neo-Paganism

A. *Gerald Gardner (1884–1964)*

1. Gerald Gardner, a British civil servant, almost single-handedly invented and popularized modern witchcraft for the Western world.

2. Gardner was supposedly initiated into witchcraft by a witch named Dorothy Clutterbuck ("Old Dorothy") in 1939.

3. He revealed some of the secrets of this supposed coven and its Mother Goddess in a novel entitled *High Magic's Aid* in 1949. It was written under a pseudonym, Gardner's magical name, "Scire."[83]

---

[79]For information on the beliefs and practices of satanism, and hence satanists, see the author's article, "The Many Faces of Satanism," in *Forward* 9, no. 2 (Fall 1986): 17–22. For a fuller treatment, see the volume *Satanism* by Bob and Gretchen Passantino in this series.

[80]*COG* information packet, "Frequently Asked Questions with Answers." Also see Jones and Matthews, *Voices from the Circle*, 23.

[81]Jones and Matthews, *Voices from the Circle*, 40.

[82]See, e.g., Cunningham, *Truth About Witchcraft*, 82, 134; Farrar, *What Witches Do*, 198; Jones and Matthews, *Voices from the Circle*, 13, 40; Starhawk, *Spiral Dance*, 32, 84.

[83]"Scire" is the present infinitive of the Latin verb *scio*, which means "to know."

4. Gardner's *Witchcraft Today* was published in 1954 following the rescinding of the witchcraft laws in England (in 1951). This work further unveiled his new goddess religion.

5. Gardner's *Meaning of Witchcraft* was published in 1959.

6. The above three works by Gardner helped to popularize witchcraft. They are still popular today among many neo-pagans.

7. Based on the theory of anthropologist, Egyptologist, folklorist, and occult dabbler, Margaret Murray (1863–1963), as well as on Gardner's own extensive occultic background, and with the help of Doreen Valiente, Gardner "crafted" modern witchcraft.[84]

   a. This type or tradition of witchcraft is termed Gardnerian witchcraft.

   b. Though some witches would strongly contest this point, contrary to his claims, Gardner did not so much uncover an ancient goddess religion as construct a new one founded on the Mother Goddess.[85]

   c. Most, if not all, of modern witchcraft and neo-paganism originates from or is significantly influenced by Gardnerian witchcraft.[86]

B. Alex Sanders (1926–1988)

1. Sanders was another early leader in the modern witchcraft movement.

2. Sanders claimed to have been initiated as a child by his grandmother into the "Old Religion." However, the facts do not support his claim.

3. It is clear that Sanders relied heavily on Gardner's work and the work of others. Although this has been denied by Sanders and others, the evidence establishes the connection.[87]

4. Based on Gardner's works and new religion, Sanders improvised his own goddess religion—his version of the "Old Religion." This is known as Alexandrian witchcraft.

C. Sybil Leek (1923–1983)

1. Leek was another very influential leader during the early modern era of witchcraft.

   a. She authored more than sixty books on witchcraft and other occultic concerns.

---

[84]For a good discussion of some of the many historical inaccuracies of Murray's view, see the volume *Satanism* in this series, by Bob and Gretchen Passantino (37–38).

[85]For documentation of this claim see Adler, *Drawing Down the Moon,* 62–64, 81–85, 93, 560; Kelly, *Crafting the Art, passim;* Luhrmann, *Persuasions,* 37, 42–44, 50, 223, 242; J. Gordon Melton, *Biographical Dictionary of American Cult and Sect Leaders* (New York: Garland, 1986), s.v. "Gardner, Gerald Brosseau," 96–97; J. Gordon Melton, *Encyclopedia of American Religions,* 3d ed. (Detroit: Gale Research, 1989), 144; Elliot Rose, *A Razor for a Goat* (Toronto: University of Toronto Press, 1962), 202–11, 218, 220; Jeffrey B. Russell, *A History of Witchcraft,* 136, 153–54; Marcello Truzzi, "Towards a Sociology of the Occult: Notes on Modern Witchcraft," in *Religious Movements in Contemporary America,* ed. Irving Zaretsky and Mark P. Leone (Princeton, N.J.: Princeton University Press, 1974), 636–37.

[86]See Melton, *Encyclopedia,* 145; Kelly, *Crafting the Art of Witchcraft,* 21–26; Kelly, *Neo-Pagan Witchcraft I,* introduction.

[87]See Adler, *Drawing Down the Moon,* 94–95, 119–20; Rosemary Ellen Guiley, *Witches and Witchcraft,* s.v. "Sanders, Alexander"; Kelly, *Neo-Pagan Witchcraft I,* introduction; Melton, *Encyclopedia,* 144, 777; Russell, *History of Witchcraft,* 154; Farrar and Farrar, *Witches Bible Compleat,* 1:15, 30; 2:244–45.

    b. She wrote an internationally syndicated column on witchcraft and the occult.

    c. She spoke widely (e.g., lectures and on television and radio) on witchcraft.

  2. Leek claimed descent from a long lineage of hereditary witches who could trace their roots in the Old Religion back to the twelfth century.

  3. While Leek may have had a long ancestry involved in some form of the occult, she was significantly impacted by Gardnerian witchcraft.

    a. She adapted Gardner's rituals and teachings.

    b. Leek, like Sanders, denied any influence from Gardnerian witchcraft.[88]

  4. She had a significant influence in popularizing witchcraft in America when she moved there in the late 1960s.

D. Raymond and Rosemary Buckland

  1. Raymond and his wife, Rosemary, traveled to England in the mid-1960s to study under Gardner. Both Raymond and Rosemary (at a later date) were initiated into Gardnerian witchcraft.

  2. Upon returning to America, the Bucklands, inspired by Gardner's occult-witchcraft museum on the Isle of Man, started their own witchcraft museum and coven on Long Island.

  3. The Bucklands were a major catalyst for the initial growth of witchcraft in America due to, among other factors, their willingness to be interviewed by the media and to talk openly about witchcraft.

  4. Currently, Raymond Buckland has written about twenty books on witchcraft or related occultic topics.

  5. Raymond Buckland founded the Seax-Wica form of witchcraft in 1973.

E. Contemporary Neo-Pagan Movement Leaders

  1. From the ideas and persons described above, other forms of neo-paganism have proliferated into the myriad types of witches, witchcraft traditions, and neo-paganism that make up the contemporary scene.

  2. Among the leaders in contemporary neo-pagan, witchcraft, and goddess movements are Margot Adler, Jim Alan, Jessie Wicker Bell (Lady Sheba), Isaac Bonewits, Raymond Buckland, Zsuzsanna (Z) Budapest, Laurie Cabot, Pauline Campanelli, Philip Carr-Gomm, Imogen Cavanagh, Chas S. Clifton, Donna Cole, Patricia Crowther, Vivianne Crowley, Scott Cunningham, Gerina Dunwich, Stewart and Janet Farrar, Selena Fox, Donald Frew, Gavin and Yvonne Frost, Marian Green, Alison Harlow, Prudence Jones, Anodea Judith, Amber K., Aidan

---

[88]See Leek, *Complete Art of Witchcraft*, 14–16, 51, 81–82; Leek, *Diary*, 28–33, 119–20, 202–6; Guiley, s.v. "Leek, Sybil"; Kelly, *Neo-Pagan Witchcraft I*, "Introduction"; Melton, *Encyclopedia*, 144, 789; J. Gordon Melton, *Encyclopedic Handbook of Cults in America* (New York: Garland, 1986), 212; Russell, *History of Witchcraft*, 148–49.

Kelly, Judy Kneitel (Lady Theos), Caitlín Matthews, Leo Martello, Morgan McFarland, Pete Pathfinder, Miriam Simos (Starhawk), Diane Stein, Paul Suliin, Doreen Valiente, Valerie Voigt, Carl Weschcke, Marion Weinstein, Morning Glory, and Otter (Tim) Zell.

VI. Vital Statistics of the Goddess and Witchcraft Movement and Other Forms of Neo-Paganism

A. *Membership Figures: Number of Neo-Pagans*
   1. The Difficulty of Determining Numbers
      a. Due to the decentralization and autonomy of witches, covens, and other neo-pagan groups, exact figures are impossible to obtain. There is no centralized authority or organization to take a census or keep track of such figures.
      b. Moreover, many neo-pagans resent and hence resist the idea of registering or determining their numbers. They view this as an invasion of their privacy.
      c. Some neo-pagans fear that such information could be used by those who are hostile toward them to persecute them.
      d. Estimates of the number of people involved in goddess worship, witchcraft, and other forms of neo-paganism can be made from subscription lists to publications or attendance at various events; however, these estimates may be inaccurate.[89]
      e. Many individuals become involved in witchcraft or other forms of neo-paganism through hearing interviews or reading books. Since its publication in 1979, Miriam Simos's (Starhawk's) *Spiral Dance: A Rebirth of the Ancient Religion of the Great Goddess* has sold more than 100,000 copies. Many people initially became involved in witchcraft or started a coven through reading this book.
   2. Approximate Numbers of Goddess Worshipers, Witches, and Other Neo-Pagans
      a. Estimates on the conservative side place the number of goddess worshipers and witches worldwide between 50,000 and 200,000.[90]
      b. Liberal estimates range between 200,000 and 300,000 for goddess worshipers and witches worldwide to upwards of 300,000 to 400,000 for all neo-pagans.

---

[89]Adler, *Drawing Down the Moon*, 107.

[90]For references on the current number of witches and other neo-pagans, see Adler, *Drawing Down the Moon*, 107–8, 418–19; Kelly, *Crafting the Art of Magic*, ix; Kelly, *Neo-Pagan Witchcraft I*, introduction; Luhrmann, *Persuasions*, 4–6. My calculations are also based on conversations and correspondence with Paul Suliin.

   c. Though the numbers for goddess worshipers, witches, and all other neo-pagans are relatively small compared to other religious movements or cults, they are growing at a steady rate.[91]

B. Literature Distribution

1. General Observations

   a. There is no centralized source of publishing or distribution of materials. However, there are several major publishers of witchcraft and other neo-pagan literature, such as Llewellyn Publications and Phoenix Publications.

   b. Dozens of journals, newsletters, newspapers, and magazines concern witches, witchcraft, and other forms of neo-paganism. Not all of the following discuss only witchcraft or the broader neo-pagan movement. Many also address the New Age Movement and/or other forms of occultism.

2. Journals, Newsletters, Newspapers, and Magazines

Asynjur, Caer Rhiannon Newsletter, The Cauldron, Circle Network News, Converging Paths, Council of the Magickal Arts, Covenant of the Goddess Newsletter, Dragonsmoke, The Druids' Progress, The Faerie Folk Newsletter, Georgian Newsletter, Goddess Rising, Golden Isis Magazine, Green Egg, Hallows, Harvest, The Hidden Path, Iron Mountain, K.A.M, Llewellyn New Times, Magickal Unicorn Messenger, Northwind Network, On Wings, Pacific Circle Newsletter, Pagana, Pagan Free Press Newsletter, Pagan Spirit Alliance Newsletter, Pagan Unity News, Panegyria, Priestless, Quest, Reclaiming Newsletter, Red Garters of California, Shadowplay, Survival, Tara, The Vigil, The Wiccan, The Wiccan Way, Wiccan Rede, The Wise Woman, Wood & Water.[92]

3. Resources

   a. Several other publications not only have articles and other information regarding witchcraft, but help goddess worshipers, witches, and other neo-pagans to network.

   b. Examples of these are the *Calendar of Events* and the *Circle Guide to Pagan Resources.*

4. Electronic media

Witches and other neo-pagans have numerous compuer bulletin boards and a strong presence on the Internet.

C. Related Groups

1. Multitudes of neo-pagan groups exist.

2. Examples include Asatru, the Church of All Worlds, the Church of Aphrodite, the Church of the Eternal Source, the Covenant of Unitarian

---

[91]My estimates on the increased number of neo-pagans are based on, among other factors, the increase in literature distribution, such as greatly increased book sales.

[92]See Adler, *Drawing Down the Moon*, 475–507, for a more complete list of publications.

Universalist Pagans, Feraferia, the New Reformed Druids of North America, Order of Bards, Ovates and Druids, the Sabaean Religious Order, Radical Faeries, and others.

D. *Contemporary Covens and Traditions*

1. There are dozens of types or traditions of contemporary witchcraft.
2. Examples include Algard, Alexandrian, American Celtic Wicca, the American Order of the Brotherhood of Wicca, Church and School of Wicca, Church of Circle Wicca, Cymry Wicca, Dianic (feminist), Gardnerian, Georgian, Maidenhill Wicca, Nova Wicca, Pecti-Wicca, Reformed Congregation of the Goddess, Seax-Wica, Temple of Wicca.[93]

E. *Witchcraft Associations and Organizations*

1. Dozens of witchcraft associations and organizations defend, network, promote, and teach witchcraft and/or related neo-pagan views.
2. These include Association of Cymmry Wicca, the Athanor Fellowship, Branches, Center of the Divine Ishtar, Circle, the Council of Isis Community, the Covenant of the Goddess, Goddess Rising, the New Wiccan Church, Our Lady of Enchantment, Our Lady of the Woods, the Pagan Federation, Pagan/Occult/Witchcraft Special Interest Group of Mensa, Reclaiming, Witches' Antidefamation League, the Witches' International Craft Associates, Witches' League for Public Awareness, Women In Constant Creative Action (W.I.C.C.A.).[94]

F. *Festivals and Gatherings*

1. There are many festivals, gatherings, and other witchcraft and neo-pagan events every year. Some are held in conjunction with other occultists such as New Agers.
2. A relatively short list includes Ancient Ways Festival, Australian Wiccan Conference, Celebration of Womanhood, Covenant of the Goddess Grand Council, Festival of Women's Spirituality, Goddess Gathering, Harvest Survival and Healing Gathering, Pacific Circle Gathering, Pagan Spirit Gathering, Samhain Festival, Samhain Seminar, Samhain Witches Ball, The Solitary Convention, The Spiral Dance.[95]

---

[93]For further information, see Adler, *Drawing Down the Moon,* 68–80, 113–30; Buckland, *Buckland's Complete Book of Witchcraft,* 225–28; Melton, *Encyclopedia,* 777–801.

[94]See Adler, *Drawing Down the Moon,* 508–35.

[95]For a more extensive list, see Adler, *Drawing Down the Moon,* 535–44.

Part II:
Theology

I. The Doctrine of Revelation

A. *Neo-Pagan Positions on Revelation Briefly Stated*

1. Revelatory truth (indeed, all truth) is based on a person's own unique, personal, subjective experiences, feelings, or intuitions. It is experientially based (existential or subjective) and relative to each person.

2. There is no one truth or one true revelation.

3. Logic plays little or no role in revelation or truth.

4. Revelatory truths are not to be conceived of as beliefs, creeds, doctrines, dogma, or theology, but rather as metaphors, myths, or poetry.

5. Revelation is often obtained through diverse divinatory techniques.

B. *Arguments Used by Neo-Pagans to Support Their Positions on Revelation*

1. Revelatory truth (indeed, all truth) is based on each person's own unique, subjective experiences, feelings, or intuitions. It is experientially based (existential or subjective) and relative to each person.

a. Everyone has his or her own revelatory truth or part of the truth.

b. One's personal experience is the final arbiter or source of revelation or truth.[1]

c. Owing to its experiential nature, each person must discover or reveal one's own revelatory truth via personal experiences. Starhawk writes, "In witchcraft, each of us must reveal our own truth."[2]

d. No one can dictate to another what truth is or tell a person that his or her views are wrong.

e. Starhawk says regarding "great men" who supposedly have the "one truth" given to the "select few," that "it supports the illusion that truth is found outside, not within, and denies the authority of experience, the truth of the senses and the body, the truth that belongs to everyone and is different for everyone."[3]

f. If something feels right—or true—to an individual, then it *is* for that person.

---

[1]See Part I, Sections II.B.4 and II.D.

[2]Starhawk, *The Spiral Dance: A Rebirth of the Ancient Religion of the Great Goddess* (San Francisco: Harper & Row, 1979), 9.

[3]Starhawk, *Dreaming the Dark: Magic, Sex and Politics,* new ed. (Boston: Beacon Press, 1988), 22; see also 37–38.

2. There is no one truth or one true revelation.[4]

   a. No one has the definitive or final word on the ultimate meaning of life or reality. At most one has a part of the truth.

   b. Every life-affirming perspective or experience must be given credence. No one can tell others in a life-affirming religion that their views are not viable, true, or right or wrong. It is true for them.

   c. What is true for one person may not necessarily be true for another.

   d. All life-affirming revelations or religions are right. Thus, there is no one way or right religion for all, no one truth.

3. Logic plays little or no role in revelation or truth.

   a. Neo-pagans tend to denigrate or deny the application of logic to revelatory truth.[5] Logic is deemed inapplicable or inadequate for discovering truth.

   b. A single logic system is inadequate to accurately or thoroughly relate reality because reality is multiple and diverse.

   c. Since there is no one logic, or logic is denigrated, dismissed, or radically restricted, contradictory views are possible.

   d. Thus, revelations can be inherently self-contradictory or can contradict other revelations or religions yet still be true or viable.

   e. Because of these and other ideas, neo-pagans sometimes assert contradictory revelatory (truth) claims.[6]

4. Revelatory truths are not to be conceived of as beliefs, creeds, doctrines, dogma, or theology, but rather as metaphors, myths, or poetry.[7]

   a. Many neo-pagans view their revelations in terms of metaphors, myths, or poetry, not as creeds, doctrine, dogma, or theology.[8]

---

[4]See, e.g., Margot Adler, *Drawing Down the Moon: Witches, Druids, Goddess-Worshippers, and Other Pagans in America Today,* rev. and exp. ed. (Boston: Beacon Press, 1986), viii, 23–25, 29–30, 169, 172, 299, 455; Philip Emmons Isaac Bonewits, *Real Magic,* rev. ed. (York Beach, Maine: Samuel Weiser, 1989), 11–14; Raymond Buckland, *Buckland's Complete Book of Witchcraft* (St. Paul: Llewellyn, 1988), 99; Scott Cunningham, *The Truth About Witchcraft Today* (St. Paul: Llewellyn, 1988), 66–67; Stewart Farrar, *What Witches Do: The Modern Coven Revealed* (London: Sphere Books, 1973), 43; T. M. Luhrmann, *Persuasions of the Witch's Craft: Ritual Magic in Contemporary England* (Cambridge: Harvard University Press, 1989), 7, 282, 290–94, 342; Starhawk, *Dreaming,* 22, 37–38; Starhawk, *Spiral Dance,* 188–90.

[5]See, e.g., Adler, *Drawing Down the Moon,* 29, 36, 43, 86, 164–65, 169–73; Luhrmann, *Persuasions,* 274–96, 301–3, 335–36, 342–44; Starhawk, *Spiral Dance,* 188–90, 197. Many neo-pagans do not deny logic per se, but attempt to radically limit its applicability. See, e.g., Adler, *Drawing Down the Moon, passim;* Janet Farrar and Stewart Farrar, *A Witches Bible Compleat* (New York: Magickal Childe, 1984), 1:18; 2:109; Luhrmann, *Persuasions,* 270–73, 282, 342–44; Starhawk, *Spiral Dance,* 188–90; Marion Weinstein, *Positive Magic: Occult Self-Help,* rev. ed. (Custer, Wash.: Phoenix, 1981), 263–67.

[6]See, e.g., Adler, *Drawing Down the Moon,* 36, 169, 172; Luhrmann, *Persuasions,* 270–73, 282, 342–44; Weinstein, *Positive Magic,* 263–67.

[7]See, e.g., Adler, *Drawing Down the Moon,* 169–73, 441–42; Prudence Jones and Caitlín Matthews, eds., *Voices from the Circle: The Heritage of Western Paganism* (Wellingborough, England: Aquarian Press, 1990), 32, 34; Luhrmann, *Persuasions,* 242–44, 273, 282, 293–96; Starhawk, *Spiral Dance,* 7–8, 23, 190, 192, 197.

[8]See Part I, Sections II.B and II.D.

    b. Aidan Kelly, for example, comments: "Knowing that all truths are merely metaphors is perhaps the greatest advantage you can have at this point in history."[9]

    c. Starhawk writes: "[Witchcraft] presents metaphors, not doctrines."[10] She also says: "Witchcraft has always been a religion of poetry, not theology. The myths, legends, and teachings are recognized as metaphors for 'That-Which-Cannot-Be-Told,' the absolute reality our limited minds can never completely know."[11]

    d. Elsewhere, Starhawk pointedly says that witchcraft "is not based on dogma or a set of beliefs" and that "it is not a belief system."[12]

5. Revelation is often obtained through diverse divinatory techniques.

    a. Different divinatory techniques are used by many neo-pagans for, among other purposes, to receive revelations (see Part I, Sections III.C–D; Part II, Section IX.B 4)

    b. Trance states can be one form of divination and lead to visions or revelations or other experiences.[13]

    c. Sybil Leek, says, "The knowledge obtained on another sphere is often exchanged and discussed when the spirit returns to the body of a person who's been in trance. It is at this highlight point that many major feats of magic, and many prophecies, are made."[14]

    d. While views vary greatly as to how or why divination works or why it is okay to practice it, neo-pagans generally have in common the belief that divination is not demonic or supernatural but that it often occurs by natural, neutral psychic powers or abilities.[15]

[9] Quoted in Adler, *Drawing Down the Moon,* 172.

[10] Starhawk, *Spiral Dance,* 197; see also 7–8, 23, 190; and Adler, *Drawing Down the Moon,* 172; Marian Green, *A Witch Alone* (London: Aquarian Press, 1991), 18–19; Luhrmann, *Persuasions,* 293–96.

[11] Starhawk, *Spiral Dance,* 7.

[12] Ibid., 2, 83.

[13] See, e.g., Adler, *Drawing Down the Moon,* 109, 168–69; Bonewits, *Real Magic,* 214, 268; Buckland, *Complete Book of Witchcraft,* 101–3; Laurie Cabot and Tom Cowan, *Power of the Witch* (New York: Dell, 1989), 16, 116, 174–75; Farrar, *What Witches Do,* 67, 153–54; Farrar and Farrar, *Witches Bible Compleat,* 2:52; Sybil Leek, *The Complete Art of Witchcraft* (New York: Signet Books, 1971), 55; Sybil Leek, *Diary of a Witch* (New York: Signet Books, 1969), 159–60, 203, 206; Kaledon Naddair, "Pictish and Keltic Shamanism," in Jones and Matthews, *Voices from the Circle,* 102; Susan Roberts, *Witches, U.S.A.* (New York: Dell, 1971), 24, 71–72, 174; Gregg Stafford, "The Medicine Circle of Turtle Island," in Jones and Matthews, *Voices from the Circle,* 87–88; Starhawk, *Spiral Dance,* 37, 46–54, 139–58; Doreen Valiente, *An ABC of Witchcraft: Past and Present* (New York: St. Martin's Press, 1973), 14, 157; Doreen Valiente, *Witchcraft for Tomorrow* (Custer, Wash.: Phoenix, 1987), 31.

[14] Leek, *Complete Art of Witchcraft,* 55.

[15] For further information on these views, see my book *Witchcraft: Exploring the World of Wicca* (Grand Rapids: Baker, 1996), chap. 3.

C. *Refutation of Arguments Used by Neo-Pagans to Support Their Positions on Revelation*

1. The Failure of Experience

    a. Mere experience—solely in and of itself—is inadequate and cannot verify religious, metaphysical, or mundane truth claims. There are numerous problems with this perspective, as follows.[16]

    b. One may have had an experience, but that does not mean that the explanation, interpretation, or significance that one attaches to it is correct. Norman Geisler says, "Since a world view is an overall interpretation of *all* facts and experiences, there is no valid way to use any particular experience within that overall interpretive framework to establish the overall framework or world view."[17] To do so would be circular reasoning.

    c. No experience, in and of itself, validates the neo-pagan worldview. To assume so is to commit the fallacy of begging the question or using circular reasoning. Without any objective or verifiable evidence, there is no compelling reason to believe the claim.

2. *True* Versus *Real* Experience(s)

    a. A critical distinction must be made between what may be called *real* versus *true* experience(s).[18]

    b. For example, we could experience the sensation of flying while dreaming. The experience could feel quite real. However, upon waking from sleep, we would realize that we were dreaming. Now, we must ask two entirely different questions: (1) Were we really flying (not just in the dream, but in real life, like a bird or plane)? (2) Did we have the experience or sensation that we were flying in the dream? The answer to (1) is no, but to (2) yes. Phenomenologically, we had the sensation or perception of the experience being true. Nonetheless, we are mistaken.

    c. The above example highlights the difference between a real versus a true experience. It would be a *real* but not a *true* experience. We had the experience of having the sensation of flying while dreaming, but we were not really flying in the external world.

    d. Experiences can feel quite real but nonetheless lead to false conclusions. We do not doubt that neo-pagans have had various

---

[16]For a more extensive treatment of these difficulties, see Norman Geisler, *Christian Apologetics* (Grand Rapids: Baker, 1976), 77–81, 138.

[17]Ibid., 78, emphasis in original.

[18]In one sense, the distinction as we have termed it is a category mistake. More correctly, one should not speak of real, true, or false experiences. Norman Geisler remarks on page 77 of *Christian Apologetics:* "Experience in the primary sense is neither true nor false. Experience is something one *has,* and truth is something one *expresses* about experience. That is, experience is a *condition* of persons but truth is a characteristic of *propositions* or expressions persons make. Hence, no experience as such is true; one simply has the experience or the awareness" (emphasis in original). However, with these points duly noted, for convenience sake, we will use our terminology.

experiences, but we deny that they prove their religious viewpoints. These are two completely different issues.

   e. It is illegitimate for neo-pagans—or others for that matter—to appeal to mere experience(s) to prove or legitimatize their religion.

3. Experience is not self-interpreting.

   a. Another problem is that experiences are not self-interpreting. It is not necessarily obvious or self-evident what the significance of an alleged experience is—if any. Most experiences are open to numerous interpretations as to why they occurred or what they mean.

   b. Depending on one's worldview (e.g., pantheistic, polytheistic, naturalistic, theistic, etc.), one can explain any given experience differently, for example, from a completely opposing worldview.

   c. For instance, a Christian, a Freudian, a behaviorist, and/or an atheist or other naturalist/materialist would likely interpret the meaning of a trance state quite differently (e.g., as demon possession, biochemical imbalance, mental illness, or something else), depending on prior assumptions or one's worldview.

   d. Some of these differing interpretations are logically mutually exclusive and thus cannot all be true (see next point).

4. Conflicting Experiences

   a. People have conflicting experiences—experiences that are mutually exclusive.

   b. For example, on the questions of whether God exists—and if so, who or what is he, she, or it—atheists, Jehovah's Witnesses, Mormons, Hare Krishnas, Hindus, and Buddhists all have conflicting experiences, all disagree. Which group are we to believe? Which experience is right? Simply appealing to or going by experiences will not help us here. They could all be wrong, but they cannot all be right.

   c. Furthermore, as Geisler comments, "if conflicting world views such as theism, pantheism and naturalism can explain all of the facts and experiences in the world, then no one of these views can have its truth claim justified by experience in face of the others. All the views have a basis in experience and a way of explaining it."[19]

5. Freedom to believe is not equivalent to the truth of that belief.

   a. Many neo-pagans confuse their ability or right to believe what they want, or to interpret a given experience as they prefer, with the notion that this freedom somehow makes their view(s) true.

   b. Neo-pagans have the right to believe whatever they want. This does not, however, mean that their views are true or that they have the right to force others to accept them as such.[20]

---

[19]Geisler, *Christian Apologetics*, 78.

[20]Alan W. Gomes treats this same issue in the context of Unitarian Universalist claims. See his volume *Unitarian Universalism*, pages 30, 34ff., in this series.

    c. Although no person can have the exact same phenomenological experience (or perception of the experience) under discussion, this does not preclude others from disagreeing with the significance, meaning, or interpretation the former proposed for it.

    d. The only element another cannot disavow is what another individual believes the experience means to him or her. Everything else is open to question.

    e. One does not have to have the exact same phenomenological experience as another to be able to verify or falsify some or all of the claims that that person attributes to it. For example, we don't need to take arsenic to know that it kills people.

6. The Undeniability of Logic

    a. For all of their rhetoric against logic, neo-pagans (or anyone else) cannot avoid using logic. It is impossible to engage in any type of coherent dialogue without using logic.

    b. One of the primary principles of logic is the law of noncontradiction. Basically, it states that no statement (proposition, assertion, etc.) can be both true and untrue (e.g., A cannot be non-A) at the same time and in the same sense.

    c. The neo-pagans' very denial that logic is applicable to their belief system is in itself dependent on logic—that is, logic had to be employed to formulate the assertion "Logic does not apply to neo-paganism." The statement "Logic does not apply" involves the distinction between "Logic *does not* apply" and "Logic *does* apply." This very distinction assumes the truth of the law of noncontradiction. Thus, the neo-pagans' position is self-refuting; their denial affirms the truth of what it is they are denying.

    d. On a practical level, one cannot avoid using logic in the real world.

        (1) Try driving to the grocery store while denying the validity of logic. (Indeed, what grocery store? The one that is and is not there?)

        (2) One cannot successfully cross railroad tracks without logic. Next time you are at a railroad crossing with an apparent train speeding down the track, imagine thinking that the train is there and it is not there. Logic is necessary for life.

7. The Biblical Position on Divination

    a. Divination (as well as spiritism, see IX below) and those who practice it are expressly condemned in the Bible (see IX.C.4 below).

    b. Since divination is not permissible, *a fortiori* it is not a legitimate source of revelation, but only of deception.

    c. In the spirit of Deuteronomy 13:1–4, we are to reject all real or imagined revelations, whether originating through divination or otherwise, that contradict the teachings of the Bible.

D. Arguments Used to Prove the Biblical Doctrine of Revelation

1. God's definitive revelation to us is in the incarnation of Jesus Christ, the second person of the Trinity (Heb. 1:1–3).

2. The Bible is a true and authoritative revelation.

   a. Jesus gives his complete approval of the Bible.

      (1) He affirmed the Old Testament's teachings and truthfulness (this would include the prohibitions on divination) and its revelatory authority (Matt. 5:17–18).

      (2) In settling disputes, Jesus consistently appealed to the Old Testament. He asserted over and over again, "It is written" (e.g., Matt. 4:4, 7, 10; 21:13; John 6:45), referring to what was written in the Old Testament. The Greek word for "it is written" is *gegraptai* and could be translated, "It is written, it stands written, it will continue—indefinitely—to stand written."

      (3) Jesus also affirmed the soon-to-be-written New Testament, which would be accomplished by the Holy Spirit working (just as with the Old Testament writers) through the New Testament writers (John 14:25–26; 15:26; 16:12–15; 2 Peter 1:20–21).

   b. The apostles likewise affirmed the Bible's authority.

      (1) Paul refers to his teachings by the inspiration of the Holy Spirit as the literal word(s) of God (1 Thess. 2:13).

      (2) Paul calls "all Scripture" (in context, the Old Testament) "God-breathed" (2 Tim. 3:15–16). Literally, the "product" (Scripture) was ultimately "the product of" God.

      (3) Paul also refers to Luke's gospel in the New Testament as "Scripture" (1 Tim. 5:18).

      (4) The apostle Peter equates Paul's New Testament writings with the "other Scriptures"—the Old Testament (2 Peter 3:15–16).

3. The Bible is a sufficient revelation.

   a. Peter tells us that God "has given us everything we need for life and godliness" (2 Peter 1:3). This provision comes through God's written revelation—the Bible.

   b. Paul also teaches the sufficiency of the Bible (2 Tim. 3:16–17).

   c. Jude 3 tell us that "the faith ... was once for all entrusted to the saints."

      (1) "The faith" (with the article "the") is not one's personal faith, but the corpus of the Christian revelation given in the Bible about spiritual things—the nature, meaning, and significance of God, humanity, creation, life, death, and so forth.

      (2) "The faith" refers to the complete and final revelation of God to us regarding spiritual issues. It is the Gospel, or good news of salvation, and all that it entails, all that one needs to know.

(3) "Once for all entrusted" indicates that the faith has *already* been revealed in the Bible. "Once for all," from the Greek word *hapax,* here means just that: once, "once for all," or for all time.[21] The word for "entrusted" or "delivered" (KJV, NASB) in the Greek text literally means "having been entrusted" or "delivered." It is a past completed action, not continuing and not to be repeated.

4. Since the revelations of neo-paganism violate or contradict the Bible, they are not true.

II. The Person of Jesus Christ

A. Neo-Pagan Positions on Jesus Christ Briefly Stated

1. Many neo-pagans do not know or care who Jesus is or what he taught.
2. Some consider Jesus a highly spiritually evolved human who simply realized his divinity or divine potential and occultic powers. As such he is an example for the rest of us.

3. Some witches consider Jesus a fellow witch who had his own coven of thirteen.
4. Others feel that Jesus, if not teaching precisely the same as neo-pagans, was at least an adept (someone proficient in occultic matters).

B. Arguments Used by Neo-Pagans to Support Their Positions on Jesus Christ

1. Many neo-pagans do not care about Jesus Christ.
   a. Many don't know or care who Jesus was, if he really lived, or what he taught. It simply is not a relevant or important question for them.
   b. Others hold that Jesus, if he lived at all, was part of a "one-truth" (i.e., patriarchal, male-dominated) oppressive and repressive religious system. Hence, they reject Jesus and his teachings.[22]
2. Jesus realized his inherent or potential divinity.
   a. Some neo-pagans believe that Jesus was a highly evolved person spiritually, who realized his divinity or divine potential. He was just one of many enlightened individuals who have lived and helped others (e.g., to recognize and develop their divine potential). Other than this, he was not really much different from us.[23]
   b. While Jesus was enlightened—aware of his (potential) divinity— he was not so in a unique sense. That is, he was not uniquely God.
      (1) Janet and Stewart Farrar write: "One of the stumbling-blocks, of course, is the Christians' insistence that Jesus was God

---

[21]Walter Bauer, *A Greek English Lexicon of the New Testament and Other Early Christian Literature* (hereafter BAG), 4th rev. and augmented ed., trans. and ed. William F. Arndt and F. Wilbur Gingrich (Chicago: University of Chicago Press, 1957), 80.

[22]See, e.g., Starhawk, *Dreaming,* 21–22; *Spiral Dance,* 101.

[23]Adler, *Drawing Down the Moon,* 454; Farrar and Farrar, *Witches Bible Compleat,* 2:122, 136, 311 (n. 2), 318.

Incarnate; that the carpenter of Nazareth . . . was in fact the creator of the Cosmos. . . . we cannot find that he ever claimed to be God. The claim seems to us to have been imposed on him later, and to be a distortion of his actual message (with which any witch or occultist would agree) that divinity resides in all of us. If it shone through him more brightly than through most other people in history, that is another matter."[24]

(2) Sybil Leek believes that we all have the "divine spark" within us. Moreover, she says, "We believe that there is a Divine Being . . . but we do not in any circumstance see a god who was like a man and who walked on the earth."[25]

3. Jesus was a witch.

a. Doreen Valiente says, "I have heard of one witch who put a portrait of Jesus in her private sanctuary because, she said, he was a great white witch and knew the secret of the coven of thirteen."[26]

b. Arnold and Patricia Crowther, asked whether they believed in Christ, said: "Yes. I believe he was a witch. He worked miracles or what we would call magic, cured people and did most things expected from a witch. He had his coven of thirteen. A high priestess, Mary Magdalane [*sic*], who had been stoned as a witch."[27]

4. Jesus was an occultist.

a. Others feel that if Jesus was not a witch or like-minded neo-pagan, then he was some other type of occultist. He at least held similar views and was an adept. He had developed his psychic (occultic) abilities and thus was a psychic healer who also practiced divination, magic/sorcery, and/or spiritism.[28]

b. Janet and Stewart Farrar remark: "Jesus knew his Cabala [Jewish occultic writings]. Some Cabalists believe that it was this knowledge, even when he was a boy, that astonished the doctors in the Temple (Luke ii, 46–7)."[29]

C. *Refutation of Arguments Used by Neo-Pagans to Support Their Positions on Jesus Christ*

1. Jesus Christ is important. Though many neo-pagans do not care much about Jesus, it is clear that they ought to.

a. It is important to have a correct view of who Jesus is.

---

[24]Farrar and Farrar, *Witches Bible Compleat*, 2:177.

[25]Leek, *Complete Art of Witchcraft*, 152.

[26]Valiente, *ABC of Witchcraft*, 14. The "secret of the coven of thirteen" refers to the belief of many neo-pagans that thirteen is the ideal number of people who can comfortably and efficiently, yet powerfully, work in the magic circle.

[27]Arnold Crowther and Patricia Crowther, *The Secrets of Ancient Witchcraft with the Witches Tarot* (Secaucus, N.J.: University Books, 1974), 164.

[28]See, e.g., Farrar and Farrar, *Witches Bible Compleat*, 2:115–16, 136, 177–78, 302, 311.

[29]Farrar and Farrar, *Witches Bible Compleat*, 2:302.

(1) One's eternal destiny depends on his/her view of Jesus, so one must have the right Jesus or the correct view of his true identity (John 8:24; 2 Cor. 11:3–4).

(2) For example, one must believe that Jesus is God incarnate, the second person of the Trinity (Matt. 7:21–23; John 1:12; 3:16; 1 John 2:23–25; 5:10–13).

(3) Other "Jesuses" and other "gospels" are counterfeits of the genuine and lead to eternal ruin (2 Cor. 11:2–4, 13–15; Gal. 1:7–9).

(4) Neo-pagans have the wrong Jesus—a counterfeit—"made in their own image"—that is, made in the likeness of their own preconceived views. In contrast, we have solid, objective evidence (in addition to the historically reliable New Testament documents)[30] of Jesus' existence and for his claims—as opposed to the mythical deities of neo-paganism.[31]

b. It is important to have a right relationship with Jesus.

(1) Eternal life is found only in *the* true Christ (John 3:16, 36; 5:21–28; 14:6; 17:1–3; 20:30–31; Acts 4:12; 1 John 2:22–25).

(2) One receives eternal life by having a relationship with Jesus as Lord and Savior, which entails responding to his claims.

(3) 1 John 5:11–12 says, "This is the testimony: God has given us eternal life, and this life is in his Son. He who has the Son has life; he who does not have the Son of God does not have life."

2. Jesus Christ is unique.

a. Jesus is qualitatively different from the rest of humanity. He *alone* is both fully God and fully man—that is, has two natures, the one fully human, the other fully divine.

b. He was not a mere man, nor was he *simply* a great teacher (see point D below).

c. Nor was he some mere mortal who realized his potential or divinity—as the rest of us supposedly can (see D.2 below).

d. Nor was or is he one of many gods and goddesses or part of a monistic divinity (see III.C–D).

---

[30]For information on the historical reliability of the New Testament, see Paul Barnett, *Is the New Testament Reliable? A Look at the Historical Evidence* (Downers Grove, Ill.: InterVarsity Press, 1986); Craig Blomberg, *The Historical Reliability of the Gospels* (Downers Grove, Ill.: InterVarsity Press, 1987); F. F. Bruce, *The New Testament Documents: Are They Reliable?* 5th rev. ed. (Grand Rapids: Eerdmans, 1960).

[31]For information on the historicity of Christ, including evidence external to the New Testament, consult Gary R. Habermas, *The Historical Jesus: Ancient Evidence for the Life of Christ* (Joplin, Mo.: College Press, 1996); F. F. Bruce, *Jesus and Christian Origins Outside the New Testament* (Grand Rapids: Eerdmans, 1974); Josh McDowell and Bill Wilson, *He Walked Among Us: Evidence for the Historical Jesus* (San Bernardino, Calif.: Here's Life, 1988); John Montgomery, *History and Christianity* (Minneapolis: Bethany House, 1965); Michael Wilkins and J. P. Moreland, *Jesus Under Fire: Modern Scholarship Reinvents the Historical Jesus* (Grand Rapids: Zondervan, 1995).

e. Jesus is unique, among other reasons, in that he alone is "the One and Only" (John 1:14), "God the One and Only, who is at the Father's side" (John 1:18) or God the Father's "one and only Son" (3:16, 18; 1 John 4:9). The Greek word translated "one and only" is *monogenes*. It literally means only, unique,[32] or "only one of its kind."[33]

f. Thus, Jesus is not merely another great human, or an individual who realized his alleged divine potential or divinity, or one of myriad gods and goddesses.

3. Jesus claimed to be incarnate deity.

a. Contrary to the claims of some neo-pagans, Jesus clearly did claim to be uniquely God, the second person of the Trinity (see D below).

b. The claims to unique deity were not "put into the mouth of Christ" or added to the Bible at a later date by overzealous devotees, as shown by the early extant manuscripts of the Greek New Testament and other relevant early literature.[34]

c. The religious leaders of Christ's day understood his claims to unique deity and wanted to kill him for it (John 5:18; 8:24–28, 57–59 [cf. Ex. 3:14]; 10:31–33; 19:7).

4. Jesus was not a witch.

a. To suggest that Jesus was a witch is not only blasphemous, but shows a profound ignorance of the biblical teachings in general and the direct teachings of Christ in particular.

b. As discussed earlier (I.D.2), Jesus completely confirmed the Old Testament teachings (e.g., Matt. 5:17–18). The Old Testament expressly forbade and condemned the beliefs/practices of neo-pagans (Deut. 18:9–12).

5. Jesus was not an occultist.

a. Jesus was not a witch nor any other type of occultist.

b. Since Jesus supported the teachings of the Old and New Testaments and they condemn occultism, Jesus condemned occultism.

c. Furthermore, as the second person of the Trinity, Jesus would not have had any need for occultic power.

D. *Arguments Used to Prove the Biblical Doctrine of the Person of Jesus Christ*

1. Jesus is fully God.

a. Jesus claimed to be God (see C.3.c above).

b. Jesus is recognized as God by others (John 1:1, 14, 18; 20:28; Rom. 9:5; Col. 2:9; Titus 1:3; 2:10, 13; 2 Peter 1:1).

---

[32]BAG, 529.

[33]D. A. Carson, *Exegetical Fallacies* (Grand Rapids: Baker, 1984), 29–30.

[34]For an introduction to the manuscript evidence, dates, and reliability of the Bible, see Norman Geisler and William Nix, *A General Introduction to the Bible*, rev. and exp. ed. (Chicago: Moody, 1986). See also notes 30–31 above.

c. Jesus is Yahweh.

(1) Yahweh (or Jehovah) is the name of God given in the Old Testament (cf. Ex. 3:4–7, 14–15). Jesus is Yahweh (as are the Father and the Holy Spirit).

(2) Verses referring to Yahweh in the Old Testament are applied to Jesus in the New Testament: Compare Psalm 34:8a with 1 Peter 2:3; Psalms 45:6–7 and 102:25–27 with Hebrews 1:8–9, 10–12; Isaiah 6:6–10 with John 12:37–41; Isaiah 8:12–13 with 1 Peter 3:14–15; Isaiah 40:28, 43:15, 44:24, and 45:18 with John 1:3, Colossians 1:16–17, and Hebrews 1:1–2, 10; Isaiah 45:21–23 with Philippians 2:9–11; and Joel 2:32 with Romans 10:13.

(3) Yahweh is the one, the only, true God (2 Chron. 15:3; Isa. 43:10–13; 44:6–8; 45:5–6, 14, 18, 21–22; Jer. 10:10).

2. Jesus is eternally God.

a. Jesus has always—from all eternity—been God (the second person of the Trinity). There was never a time when he was not God. He has been, is, and always will be God.

b. One of God's unique attributes is eternal existence (Deut. 33:27; Neh. 9:5; Pss. 45:6; 90:2; 102:25–27; Isa. 40:28; Rom. 16:26; 1 Tim. 1:17; 6:15–16; Heb. 1:10–12; Rev. 4:8–9).

c. The Old Testament contains passages regarding Christ Jesus and his eternality (Isa. 9:6; Mic. 5:2).

d. Jesus already existed and was God before the beginning of creation and time (John 1:1–2; 17:5).[35]

e. Christ Jesus created *all* that has been created (Ps. 102:25; John 1:1–3, 10; 1 Cor. 8:6; Col. 1:16–17; Heb. 1:2, 10). Everything that has been made or has come into existence, he made. If he came into existence at one point in time, he would have had to make himself.

3. Jesus is fully human.

a. Not only is Jesus fully divine, but he is also fully human—that is, Jesus has a complete human nature.

b. Jesus *became* human at his incarnation. Thus, Jesus is fully God (from all eternity) and (became) fully human (Luke 2:4; John 1:1, 14, 18; Rom. 1:1–5; 9:5; Phil. 2:5–11; Heb. 2:14).

4. Because of who Jesus is, he is trustworthy.

a. Being God, the second person of the Trinity, Jesus cannot lie or err, but only speaks truth.

b. Jesus, speaking to the veracity of the Bible (Matt. 5:17–18), affirms the condemnation of all occultic practices (Deut. 18:9–12).

---

[35]See Leon Morris, "The Gospel According to John," in *The New International Commentary on the New Testament,* ed. F. F. Bruce (Grand Rapids: Eerdmans, 1971), 72–74; Merrill C. Tenney, "John–Acts" in *The Expositor's Bible Commentary,* Frank E. Gaebelein, gen. ed. (Grand Rapids: Zondervan, 1981), 9:29.

III. The Doctrine of God

A. *Four Primary Neo-Pagan Positions on God Briefly Stated*

1. Many neo-pagans are polytheists.
2. Many neo-pagans are pantheists.
3. Many neo-pagans are panentheists.
4. Many are a combination of the above and/or hold other views.
5. Many neo-pagans believe that what most nonpagans term evil is part of the very nature of the divine being(s), goddess(es) and/or god(s).

B. *Arguments Used by Neo-Pagans to Support Their Positions on God*

1. Many neo-pagans are polytheists.[36]

   a. The witch Margot Adler writes, *"While most Neo-Pagans disagree on almost everything, one of their most important* principles is polytheism."[37]

   b. Many neo-pagans believe in multiple deities—gods and goddesses, or a pantheon (generally at least the Goddess and the Horned God).

   c. These neo-pagans view polytheism as the perspective that best corresponds to their understanding of reality.

2. Many neo-pagans are pantheists.[38]

   a. For these neo-pagans, all of creation is divine. All is god, god is all. Hence, divinity is immanent in nature and humanity: creation and humanity are divine.[39]

   b. Starhawk, for example, refers to "the world, which is divine, and to the divine, which is the world. . . . All things are divine, are manifestations of the Goddess."[40]

   c. The "Declaration of Principles" states, "[Neo-]Pagans recognize the divinity of Nature and of all living things."[41]

---

[36]See, e.g., Adler, *Drawing Down the Moon*, viii, ix, 4, 10, 23–38, 112; Farrar, *What Witches Do*, 40; Farrar and Farrar, *Witches Bible Compleat*, 2:113, 309; Jones and Matthews, Introduction, *Voices from the Circle*, 33; Aidan Kelly, *Crafting the Art of Magic, Book I: A History of Modern Witchcraft, 1939–1964* (St. Paul: Llewellyn, 1991), 5–6; Leek, *Complete*, 42–44, 50, 153; Starhawk, *Dreaming*, 38; Weinstein, *Positive Magic*, 68, 69.

[37]Adler, *Drawing Down the Moon*, 24, emphasis in original.

[38]See ibid., ix, 4, 25, 101, 122; Cabot and Cowan, *Power of the Witch*, 13; Farrar, *What Witches Do*, 194; Jones and Matthews, Introduction, *Voices from the Circle*, 15, 35, 40; Leek, *Complete Art of Witchcraft*, 50, 110, 155; Russell, *A History of Witchcraft*, 158; Starhawk, *Spiral Dance*, 8–9, 24, 27, 29, 78.

[39]See, e.g., Adler, *Drawing Down the Moon*, ix, 101; Cabot and Cowan, *Power of the Witch*, 13, 295, 302; Cunningham, *Truth About Witchcraft*, 73, 83, 99; Farrar, *What Witches Do*, 83, 198; Jones and Matthews, *Voices from the Circle*, 15, 35, 40; Leek, *Complete Art of Witchcraft*, 48, 148, 152, 155, 190; Starhawk, *Spiral Dance*, 8, 22, 27, 29, 84–85, 102, 197; Starhawk, *Truth or Dare: Encounters with Power, Authority, and Mystery* (San Francisco: Harper San Francisco, 1987), 7, 315, 318; Weinstein, *Positive Magic*, 23, 25, 40, 71, 108, 205.

[40]Starhawk, *Spiral Dance*, 24, 29.

[41]Jones and Matthews, Introduction, *Voices from the Circle*, 40.

d. Adler asserts, "For many [Neo-]Pagans, *pantheism* implies much the same thing as animism. It is a view that divinity is inseparable from nature and that deity is immanent in nature."[42]

e. It would follow that if all is god (a manifestation of the Goddess/God), or god is all, then all of creation (e.g., nature and humanity) is divine.

f. In light of the above, neo-pagans in some sense revere nature.

g. Jones and Matthews remark, "The new Pagans are also explicitly Nature-worshippers, enthusiastically espousing the root meaning of their name; *pagani*, of the countryside."[43]

3. Many neo-pagans are panentheists.[44]

a. Many neo-pagans are panentheists (whether they know it or not).

b. Panentheism is the view that the world is a manifestation of, or is contained in, the divine. While the divine is immanent in the world, it still transcends the universe to some degree. As the human body is to the mind or soul, analogously, the universe is to the divine. All that exists is part of and imbued with divinity yet is not the totality of the divinity.

c. Paul Suliin says: "All things in the universe are manifestations of Divinity, and as such are held to be sacred and venerable. The Gods are both immanent beings and parts of a transcendent whole."[45]

4. Many neo-pagans hold a combination of the above views or other views. Adler says of neo-pagans, "They are usually polytheists or animists or pantheists, or two or three of these things at once."[46]

5. Many neo-pagans believe that what most nonpagans term "evil" is part of the very nature of the divine being(s), goddess(es), or god(s).

a. Most neo-pagans regard "evil" as a vital, indeed necessary, part of the divine being(s), and also of the life process generally.

b. Many (most?) neo-pagans do not believe that evil is really evil per se. It is simply one pole of the duality in the divine being(s)—e.g., good/evil, light/dark, positive/negative—and the life process.

c. No prescriptive value is placed on what some neo-pagans term the dark side of the divine being(s). It is merely descriptive (e.g., good/evil, light/dark, positive/negative).

d. In describing the views of witches (and other neo-pagans), Erica Jong writes: "Satanists . . . accept the Christian duality between good and evil; pagans do not. . . . Pagans see good and evil as intimately allied, in fact, indivisible. They conceive of deities as having

---

[42]Adler, *Drawing Down the Moon,* 25.
[43]Jones and Matthews, Introduction, *Voices from the Circle,* 13; see also "The Pagan Federation," 221.
[44]Correspondence with Paul Suliin.
[45]Correspondence with Paul Suliin.
[46]Adler, *Drawing Down the Moon,* 4.

several aspects—creation, destruction, sustenance—rather than externalizing all destruction and destructiveness ('evil') in the form of devils."[47]

e. Weinstein writes: *"The witch philosophy of Light and Dark*: No duality exists between good and evil. The One Power over all is neither good nor bad; it transcends qualitative thought."[48]

C. *Refutation of Arguments Used by Neo-Pagans to Support Their Positions on God*

1. Biblical Critiques of Polytheism

   a. There is only one God (Deut. 4:35, 39; 6:4; Isa. 43:10–11; 44:6–8; 45:5–6, 14, 18, 21–22; 46:9; 1 Tim. 1:17; James 2:19; Jude 25).

   b. No other gods (or goddesses) existed before Yahweh; nor will any come into existence after him (Isa. 43:10).

   c. In Isaiah 44:6, 8; 45:5–6, 14, 21; and 46:9 we are told that there are no other gods (or goddesses) existing besides Yahweh.

   d. Therefore, there is only one God—Yahweh (2 Sam. 7:22; Neh. 9:6; Ps. 86:10; Isa. 37:16, 20; 43:10–11; Jer. 10:10).

   e. Even though there is only one true God by nature (1 Cor. 8:4–6), there are many false or so-called "gods," "lords," or "goddesses" (Gal. 4:8).

   f. The false gods and goddesses are expressly denounced. They are referred to in a very derogatory manner (1 Kings 11:5, 7; 2 Kings 23:13; Jer. 11:13).

   g. Those who worship the false gods and goddesses are also denounced (Ex. 23:13; Deut. 4:3, 19; 8:19–20; 16:21–22; Josh. 24:20; Judg. 2:10–15; 3:7–8; 10:6–16; 1 Kings 11:32–33; Ps. 81:8–9; Jer. 11:9–17).

2. Biblical Critiques of Pantheism and Panentheism[49]

   a. Only Yahweh is God or divine (2 Sam. 7:22; 2 Kings 19:15; Neh. 9:6; Ps. 86:8–10; Isa. 37:20; 43:10; 45:5–6, 18; 46:9).

   b. Yahweh (God) is the creator of everything. Nonetheless, he is separate or distinct from his creation(s).

      (1) Yahweh has made all that exists—for example, angels, the heavens, humans and all other living life-forms, and the world (Gen. 1:1; 14:19, 22; Deut. 32:6; Neh. 9:6; Ps. 33:6; Isa. 40:26–28; 42:5; 44:24; 45:12; Matt. 19:4; Acts 14:15; 17:24; Heb. 1:10; 11:3; Rev. 4:11; 14:7).

---

[47]Erica Jong, *Witches* (New York: Abrams, 1981), 52.

[48]Marion Weinstein, *Positive Magic*, 88, emphasis in original; see also 87–88. See also *Earth Magic: A Dianic Book of Shadows*, rev. and exp. ed. (Custer, Wash.: Phoenix, 1986), 55–56.

[49]While there are substantive differences between pantheism and panentheism, in regard to our concerns they can be treated together.

      (2) However, Yahweh is not identical to his creation. He is distinguished from it (e.g., the heavens, the earth, and people—Ps. 113:5–6; Isa. 40:22–25).

      (3) The Bible contrasts Yahweh with his creation (Ps. 102:25–27; Rom. 1:25).

      (4) Nothing (angels, the heavens, humans, the earth, etc.) can be compared with God (Pss. 89:6; 113:5–6; Isa. 40:18, 25; 46:5).

      (5) If any aspect of creation was divine or part of the divinity, then it could and should be compared with God, since it would be an aspect of the divine. However, Scripture never does this and, in fact, teaches the opposite. Creation can only be incompatibly contrasted, not congruously compared with God.

  c. We are to worship Yahweh (God) only, not creation.

      (1) We are to worship Yahweh. Indeed, we are commanded to worship him alone (Ex. 23:25–26; Deut. 6:13; 2 Kings 17:39; Ps. 99:5, 9; Luke 4:8; Heb. 12:28; Rev. 14:7; 22:9).

      (2) We are forbidden to worship what is not God, or so-called "gods"—aspects of creation (Ex. 20:3–5; 34:14; Deut. 6:13–14; 8:19–20).

      (3) For example, we are forbidden to worship angels (Matt. 4:8–10; Luke 4:5–8; Col. 2:18; Rev. 19:10; 22:8–9) and humans (Acts 10:25–26; 12:20–23; 14:11–15).

      (4) If any aspect of creation (angels, the heavens, humans, animals, earth, etc.) was God or divine, we could and should worship it. Biblically we would be commanded to. However, this is categorically forbidden. We are not to worship any of creation. Therefore, none of creation is God or divine, which means that pantheism and panentheism are false views of reality.

3. The Problem of Evil for Polytheism

  a. There are numerous pivotal problems relative to evil for polytheism.

  b. Examples of evil include persons being crippled, maimed, or tortured; and natural disasters, such as earthquakes, floods, and hurricanes.

  c. The problem of evil pertains to the origin and existence of evil. The chief questions for our purposes are, given the alleged existence of the divine being(s), what is the source or origin of evil, why does it exist, and will it ever end?

  d. Many neo-pagans believe that the problem of evil does not apply to their understanding of reality.[50] For example, many neo-pagans deny that evil really is evil.

  e. Yet the problem of evil for neo-pagans comes into play given the alleged nature of the goddess(es)/god(s).

---

[50] See chap. 8 in my book *Witchcraft.*

(1) For example, are not the goddess(es)/god(s) responsible for the evil they have birthed? Are they not the alleged source of life for good or ill? Is this not allegedly their world, their creation? The goddess(es)/god(s) are culpable for what they have created—their catastrophes or calamities, the chaos they cause. They are responsible for evil; it is their atrocity.

(2) While many neo-pagans attempt to deny that evil is really evil, it is intuitive to human nature, since we are made in the image of God, that evil occurrences really are evil or wrong and not just unpleasant or unfortunate aspects of life.

(3) Since many neo-pagans hold that the goddess(es) and god(s) participate in the principle of polarity (e.g., light/dark, positive/negative), they contain, among other things, good and what most nonpagans call evil.

(4) Moreover, since the goddess(es) and god(s) both contain and in some sense condone evil, how could they ever put an end to it? They could only end evil if they themselves ceased to exist—that is, evil will never cease to exist until they do.

(5) Since most neo-pagans do not believe that the goddess(es)/god(s) are omniscient (all-knowing), omnipotent (all-powerful), and/or omnibenevolent (completely good), they cannot put an end to evil. They possess their attributes to a greater or lesser degree, but none to perfection. They are beings of greater or lesser virtue who are unable to end the existence of evil.

f. Thus, the goddess(es) and god(s) cannot and/or will not end the existence of evil, because (1) it is part of their nature, (2) they condone evil as "good" or necessary for their own existence and supposedly for life on the whole, and (3) they are too inept to end it.

g. Therefore, evil will never cease to exist in this world (or in any other possible or future world), and they are responsible for it.

4. The Problem of Evil for Pantheism and Panentheism

a. The problem of evil here is similar to the problem of evil in regard to polytheism. Evil undeniably originates, emanates, or follows from the divinity's very nature, since it is the originator or source of all. The divinity is and always will be the source of evil.

b. In a pantheistic or panentheistic universe, creation and evil are simultaneous and synonymous.[51] Evil is a component, or aspect, of the divinity itself. Therefore, evil definitely and directly originates from the divinity, since evil is a component of its being and everything stems from it.

---

[51]Mark C. Albrecht, *Reincarnation: A Christian Critique of a New Age Doctrine* (Downers Grove, Ill.: InterVarsity Press, 1982), 107.

c. If good and evil are both necessary,[52] how could evil cease to exist? It is a necessary life component of the pantheistic or panentheistic world.

d. Furthermore, since the divinity is eternal, evil is eternal. The only way for evil to cease to exist is for the divinity to cease to exist. But this is not a possibility in a pantheistic or panentheistic universe.

e. Therefore, why should we not value "evil" if it is just one alleged polarity that is necessary for life.[53]

f. Since the divinity transcends good and evil, and since all is One[54]— the divinity—should we not also transcend good and evil? If not, why not? If evil is not evil for the divinity, then why should it be for you or me? Yet we know that the concepts of good and evil do apply to us and there would be chaos—rank evil—if we consistently acted as if they did not.

D. Arguments Used to Prove the Biblical Doctrine of God

1. God's moral perfections set him apart from neo-pagan deities.

a. Unlike neo-pagan deities, God is completely holy (Lev. 11:44–45; 19:1–2; Isa. 6:3; 1 Peter 1:15–16; Rev. 4:8; 15:2–4; 16:5). God is completely without sin, darkness, or the "negative" (Deut. 32:4; Ps. 92:15; Zeph. 3:5). He is complete light (Ps. 104:2; 1 Tim. 6:15–16; 1 John 1:5).

b. God is perfect—relative to every aspect of his nature or being— for example, in his counsel or morality (Deut. 32:4; 2 Sam. 22:31; Matt. 5:48).

c. God is completely good (Pss. 25:8; 86:5; 100:5; Jer. 33:11; Acts 14:17).

d. All of God's actions and decrees are just and righteous (Deut. 32:4; Pss. 11:7; 119:137; 145:17; Isa. 45:21; Rev. 15:2–4; 16:5–7).

e. God will not condone sin and unrighteousness (Ps. 5:4–6; Hab. 1:13; James 1:13).

f. While God is completely holy and righteous, and will judge unrepentant sin, he is nonetheless a merciful and forgiving God (Prov. 28:13; Isa. 55:7; Dan. 9:9; Mic. 7:18–19; Acts 2:38). He is gracious and compassionate (2 Chron. 30:9; Neh. 9:17, 31; Pss. 86:15; 103:1–18; 116:5; 145:8–9; Joel 2:12–14) and good to all of his creation (Ps. 145:9, 13, 15–17; Matt. 5:45; Acts 14:17).

---

[52]Cabot and Cowan, *Power of the Witch,* 159–61; Farrar, *What Witches Do,* 43; Farrar and Farrar, *Witches Bible Compleat,* 2:75, 107, 111, 113, 195; Starhawk, *Dreaming,* 40; Starhawk, *Spiral Dance,* 27, 28, 29–30, 78, 98–99, 189, 197; Weinstein, *Positive Magic,* 87, 88, 249, 250.

[53]Weinstein, *Positive Magic,* 87–88, 249; Farrar and Farrar, *Witches Bible Compleat,* 2:107, 111, 113, 195; Jong, *Witches,* 52; Leek, *Complete Art of Witchcraft,* 29–34; Beth Neilson and Imogen Cavanaugh, "She of Many Names," in Jones and Matthews, *Voices from the Circle,* 122–23; Starhawk, *Dreaming,* 40; Starhawk, *Spiral Dance,* 28, 29–30, 80–81, 98–99; Weinstein, *Earth Magic,* 55–56, 60.

[54]For example, Weinstein tells us that "no duality exists between good and evil. The One Power over all is neither good nor bad; it transcends qualitative thought" (*Positive Magic,* 88).

2. God's nonmoral attributes also set him apart from neo-pagan deities.

    a. God is independent. He is not dependent on anything or anyone—such as angels or humans—for anything (Job 41:11; Pss. 24:1; 50:9–12; Acts 17:25). Everything and everyone belongs to God.

    b. God is the sovereign ruler over all that exists (2 Sam. 7:22; Dan. 4:17, 35; Isa. 14:24; 43:13; Jer. 32:17; Ezek. 36:7; Acts 4:24). He does as he pleases (Ps. 135:6; Isa. 46:10–11).

    c. God is immutable. He does not change his essential nature, mind, or will (Num. 23:19; 1 Sam. 15:29; Ps. 33:11; Mal. 3:6; James 1:17).

    d. God is omniscient—all-knowing (Job 37:16; Ps. 147:4–5; Isa. 40:28; 46:9–10; Rom. 11:33; Heb. 4:13; 1 John 3:20).

    e. God is omnipotent—all-powerful (Jer. 32:17, 27; Matt 19:26; Mark 14:36; Rev. 19:6).

    f. God is omnipresent (Ps. 139:7–10; Jer. 23:23–24).

    g. God is transcendent (Deut. 4:39; 2 Chron. 2:6; Ps. 113:5–6).

    h. God is immanent (Deut. 4:7; Ps. 139:7–10; Jer. 23:23–24; Acts 17:27–28).

3. The biblical God is personal.[55] The one true God is not impersonal like the "god" of pantheism or panentheism.

    a. God feels or has a full range of emotions (Gen. 6:6; Ex. 20:5–6; Pss. 5:5; 11:5; Isa. 62:4–5; Ezek. 5:13).

    b. God loves (Ps. 107:1, 8; Jer. 31:3; Hos. 2:19; 1 John 4:16).

    c. God hates or feels anger (Pss. 5:5; 11:5; Lam. 2:1–3; Ezek. 5:13; Zeph. 3:8).

    d. God, in a good sense, is jealous (Ex. 20:5; 34:14; Deut. 4:24; 6:15; Josh. 24:19; Nah. 1:2; 1 Cor. 10:21–22).

    e. God thinks and knows (1 Sam. 2:3; Ps. 139:1–4; Jer. 29:11; Acts 1:24; 1 John 3:20).

    f. God exercises judgment (1 Chron. 28:9; Prov. 5:21; 16:2; Isa. 1:24–25; Jer. 17:10; Rom. 2:16).

    g. God has a will (Isa. 46:10–11; Acts 13:2; Rom. 12:2; 1 Thess. 4:3; 1 Peter 2:15).

    h. God directly interacts with and relates to people (Gen. 3:8; 6:13, 18; 12:1–7; 26:24; 28:13–15; Ex. 24:9–17; 33:7–11; Josh. 1:1–9; 2 Cor. 6:16; 1 John 1:1; Rev. 21:3).

4. God is not his creation.

    a. While God is immanent and is the creator of all, nonetheless, he is separate or distinct from it (Acts 17:24; see III.C.2.b above).

---

[55]For a more complete list of God's attributes of personality, see the *Topical Analysis of the Bible*, Walter Elwell, gen. ed. (Grand Rapids: Baker, 1991).

b. Thus, while creation as such is good (Gen. 1:31; 1 Tim. 4:4), it is not God or divine (Rom. 1:20–25).

c. Creation reflects God's glory, abilities, appreciation of beauty and variety, brilliance, creativity, majesty, power, and so on, but nevertheless is not the creator.

5. Conclusion

a. Only the true triune God revealed in the Bible is worthy of worship (Ps. 96:4–9; Rev. 4:11). This is because of who he is by nature and what he has done (e.g., created everything).

b. God has revealed himself to us. Thus, through Jesus, God is knowable and approachable (Heb. 1:1–2).

IV. The Doctrine of Humanity

A. *Neo-Pagan Positions on Humanity Briefly Stated*
   1. Humans are divine or potentially so.
   2. People are basically good.

B. *Arguments Used by Neo-Pagans to Support Their Positions on Humanity*
   1. Many believe that humans are divine or potentially so: divinity is immanent in humanity.[56]

      a. It would follow, for example, if all is god (divine) and god is all, or a manifestation of the goddess/god, then all of creation, including humanity, is divine (or part of the divinity).[57]

      b. Sybil Leek says, "Because all things spring from the Divine Being, we as men partake of the nature of the divinity."[58]

      c. One neo-pagan group greets its female and male members respectively: "Thou art Goddess," "Thou art God."[59]

      d. Adler asserts, "No matter how diverse Neo-Pagans' ideas about deities, almost all of them have some kind of 'Thou Art God/dess' concept."[60]

   2. People are basically good.

      a. By this is meant that people are not basically evil or sinful; they do not have a fallen nature or a nature with an inherent proclivity to do evil. (Thus, they are not in need of salvation as a Christian would understand that concept [see VI.A–B and VII.A–B below].)

      b. This does not mean that people never do bad or wrong things, or that some individuals have not chosen evil lifestyles, but rather

---

[56]Adler, *Drawing Down the Moon,* ix, 24–38, 166, 167, 173, 202; Vivianne Crowley, "The Initiation," in Jones and Matthews, *Voices from the Circle,* 80. See also n. 39.

[57]See above, Section III.B.2.a–e.

[58]Leek, *Complete Art of Witchcraft,* 155.

[59]Adler, *Drawing Down the Moon,* 25, 166.

[60]Ibid., 202.

that this is not true of all human beings and that we cannot generalize about humans in this manner.

   c. Human nature is seen either as neutral toward good or evil or having a propensity toward good.

C. *Refutation of Arguments Used by Neo-Pagans to Support Their Positions on Humanity*

   1. Humans are not divine, nor are they potentially so. This is shown by the striking contrast between God and human beings.

     a. As previously shown, Yahweh is the only one, true God (III.C.1).

     b. Yahweh is not his creation—you, me, or anyone or anything else (III.C.2; D.4).

     c. God is separate or distinct from and unlike humanity (Num. 23:19; 1 Sam. 15:29; Isa. 31:3; Hos. 11:9). That is, God (except for Jesus after his incarnation) does not have a human nature.

     d. Yahweh is God from all eternity (Pss. 90:2; 93:2; 1 Tim. 1:17). God is eternal. Humanity was created by God (Gen. 1:27; 2:7; Deut. 4:32; Ps. 100:3; Matt. 19:4; Col. 1:16; Rev. 4:11). Since we were created by God, we are not eternal beings. There was a time when we did not exist. God, however, has always existed.

     e. God is perfect, holy, without sin (III.D.1.a–d). We are imperfect (in and of ourselves), unholy, sinful (Job 4:17; Isa. 64:6; Rom. 3:9–19, 23).

     f. Yahweh is omnipresent (III.D.2.f), while humanity is limited to one place at a time (Acts 17:26).

     g. Yahweh is omniscient (III.D.2.d). Humanity is quite limited in knowledge (Job 8:9; Eccl. 8:17; 1 Cor. 3:18).

     h. Yahweh is omnipotent (III.D.2.e). His strength never fails or fades (Isa. 40:28). Humanity is frail and will die (Gen. 6:3; Job 14:1–5; Pss. 39:4–6; 103:13–16; Isa. 2:22; Dan. 4:35).

     i. There is an infinite difference between God and humanity (Job 11:7–9; 36:26; Isa. 40:25–26; 55:8–9). God is infinite, humanity finite—limited.

     j. Only Yahweh has life in himself or is self-existent (Ex. 3:14; John 5:26; Acts 3:15; 17:25; 1 Tim. 6:15–16).

       (1) Life for all other living beings is derived from God, is contingent upon him, not themselves (Gen. 2:7; 1 Sam. 2:6; Neh. 9:6; Job 12:10; Ps. 104:29; Isa. 42:5; Dan. 5:23; Acts 17:25; Col. 1:16; 1 Tim. 6:13; Rev. 4:11).

       (2) Thus, humans were created by God and are dependent on him for their life or existence and are inferior to him.[61]

       (3) Thus, humans are not self-existent or divine.

---

[61]See Elwell, *Topical Analysis*, 317–19.

2. People are not "basically good"; rather, they are sinful by nature (Rom. 3:9–19, 23).

 a. This does not mean that to be human as such is bad or sinful. Indeed, to be human in and of itself is essentially good (see IV.D.1–3 below). God directly created our human nature.

 b. However, since the fall of humanity, human nature, which is good in and of itself, has become radically marred by sin (see VI.C–D below). Thus, now all humans have a corrupted human nature.

 c. Human nature, in and of itself (since the Fall), has a proclivity toward evil and a hatred of the true God (see VI.C below).

D. Arguments Used to Prove the Biblical Doctrine of Humanity[62]

1. We were created by God (IV.C.1.j above).

2. We are made in God's image (Gen. 1:26–27; 9:6; 1 Cor. 11:7; James 3:9).

 a. We share with God what are termed his communicable attributes (e.g., creativity, emotions, morality, rationality, and volition).

 b. We have the capability to create or invent: from reproducing offspring, to art, literature, music, mechanical inventions, and so on (Ex. 28:3; 31:1–11; 35:25–26, 30–35; 36:1–8; 1 Chron. 22:15–16; 25:6–7; Ps. 45:1).

 c. We are conscious or self-reflective beings (Rom. 9:1; 2 Cor. 1:12).

 d. We have emotions (e.g., anger, happiness, grief, love, pity, sorrow).

 e. We make moral judgments/decisions (Deut. 30:15–20; Josh. 24:14–15; Matt. 5:19).

 f. We have moral affections.[63]

 g. We have the ability to reason or think (Isa. 1:18; Acts 17:2–3, 17, 18:4).

 h. We have volition or a will: the ability to choose or make certain decisions (Gen. 23:8; John 1:13; 1 Cor. 7:37).

 i. In these senses we are made in the image of God. We are *not* made so in the sense of his incommunicable attributes (e.g., eternality, omnipotence, omnipresence, omniscience, and divinity).

3. Humans have inherent value because of being made in God's image.

 a. Humans are superior to plants or animals (Gen. 1:28; 9:1–3; Matt. 10:29–31; 12:11–12).

 b. Humanity is the crown of God's creation (Pss. 8:5–6; 139:14).

4. We were made for eternal relationship and fellowship with the personal loving God of the universe (John 3:16; 1 John 1:1–3).

5. Despite all this, humanity,one and all, is a corrupted creation—radically contaminated, infected, or marred by sin (see VI.C–D below).

---

[62]For more references on the biblical view, see Elwell, *Topical Analysis,* 303–65, 372–401, 446.
[63]See Elwell, *Topical Analysis,* 310–15.

V. The Doctrine of Magic/Sorcery

A. *Neo-Pagan Positions on Magic/Sorcery Briefly Stated*

1. Magic/sorcery and the development of psychic abilities are important to many neo-pagans.

2. For most neo-pagans, magic is not involved with the supernatural (which allegedly does not exist in the first place), but for many is considered to be "superscience." That is, magic/sorcery for most neo-pagans is natural, part of the makeup of reality.

3. Magic/sorcery is morally neutral, neither good nor evil in and of itself.

4. Neo-pagans do not call on demons to aid in their magical practices.

5. Some neo-pagans argue that magic is taught or approved of by the Bible and/or Jesus.

B. *Arguments Used by Neo-Pagans to Support Their Positions on Magic/Sorcery*

1. The development of psychic potential or abilities is given a prominent place by many neo-pagans (see Part I, Section III.F). Magical or occultic practices (the occultic arts and technologies) that result from psychic activities include such things as speaking incantations, making potions, raising psychic power, (for some) performing sex magic, and casting spells (see Part I, Section III.E).

2. For most neo-pagans, magic is not involved with the supernatural (which allegedly does not exist), but for many is considered to be "superscience." That is, magic/sorcery for most neo-pagans is natural.

   a. For many neo-pagans, the occult and magic/sorcery are not involved with the supernatural, but with avant-garde science.[64]

   b. Magic/sorcery is simply a constituent or construct of nature—the natural order of life, reality, or the universe.[65] Thus, magic is not supernatural, but natural, since it is a part of or contained within nature.

   c. Sybil Leek says: "I can see little difference in Magic and science, except to have the opinion that Magic is one step ahead of science."[66]

   d. Tim Zell states: "Magic is the science you don't understand, the science you don't take for granted. ... If you have a theory to explain

---

[64]See, e.g., Adler, *Drawing Down the Moon,* 8, 154–55, 309, 369–70; Bonewits, *Real Magic,* 33, 34–70, 137–40, 197; Cabot and Cowan, *Power of the Witch,* 142–68, 172, 174–76, 200, 298; Cunningham, *Truth About Witchcraft,* 3, 23–24; Farrar and Farrar, *Witches Bible Compleat,* 2:110; Amber K., "Beginning True Magick," in Aidan Kelly, ed., *Neo-Pagan Witchcraft I* (New York: Garland, 1990), 252; Starhawk, *Spiral Dance,* 18; Doreen Valiente, *Natural Magic* (Custer, Wash.: Phoenix, 1991), 9; Weinstein, *Positive Magic,* 214.

[65]See, e.g., Adler, *Drawing Down the Moon,* 6, 7–8, 41, 102, 154–55, 369–70; Cunningham, *Truth About Witchcraft,* 18, 23–25; Farrar and Farrar, *Witches Bible Compleat,* 2:110; Luhrmann, *Persuasions,* 141; Leo Martello, *Witchcraft: The Old Religion* (Secaucus, N.J.: Citadel Press, 1973), 12; Starhawk, *Spiral Dance,* 132; Valiente, *ABC of Witchcraft,* 270; Weinstein, *Positive Magic,* 214.

[66]Leek, *Diary,* 144.

51

something, it gets called science. If people don't understand something, or lack a theory to explain it, they label it 'magic.'"[67]

e. Thus, for most neo-pagans, magic has nothing to do with the supernatural or silly superstitions.

3. Magic/sorcery is morally neutral, neither good nor evil in and of itself.

a. Most neo-pagans view magic as being morally neutral.[68] It is neither morally good nor bad in and of itself, though it can be used for good or bad ends. But this depends on a person's use of it.

b. For some neo-pagans, the motive, along with the means or methods and the goals or purposes, determines the rightness or wrongness of a given magical practice.

(1) Bonewits writes: "Magic is a science and an art, and as such has nothing to do with morals or ethics. Morals and ethics come in only when we decide to apply the results of our research and training. *Magic is about as moral as electricity.*"[69]

(2) Sybil Leek says: "It is the individual who decides which way occult forces will be used; for good, as in witchcraft, or for destructive purposes, as in black magic. . . . But never forget that the force that comes down to you comes from the same source, whether you have the potential to be an Aleister Crowley or Jesus Christ."[70]

c. Thus, in and of itself the practice of magic is not wrong or immoral.

4. Neo-pagans do not call on demons to aid in their magical practices.

a. Some neo-pagans believe that magic (in whole or in part) is accomplished without the intervention of spirits (if they believe they exist in the first place).[71] That is, neo-pagans of this persuasion do not invoke spirits in their magical practices.

b. Other neo-pagans argue that various types of spirits may or may not exist and may or may not be involved in magic, but demons or other evil spirits—if they exist at all—are not involved in magic. Amber K., for instance, insists: "Magick is not the medieval art of summoning 'demons' to do one's will."[72]

c. Since most neo-pagans do not believe that the devil exists, they do not believe that he is somehow involved with magic.

---

[67]Quoted in Adler, *Drawing Down the Moon,* 309.

[68]See, e.g., Adler, *Drawing Down the Moon,* 8, 154–60; Bonewits, *Real Magic,* 116–17, 200; Farrar, *What Witches Do,* 46; Gavin Frost and Yvonne Frost, *The Magic Power of Witchcraft* (West Nyack, N.Y.: Parker, 1976), 7; Leek, *Complete Art of Witchcraft,* 64–65, 75–76, 154–55; Roberts, *Witches, U.S.A.,* 30, 33–34, 203; Valiente, *Natural Magic,* 11, 69; Weinstein, *Earth Magic,* 56, 60; Weinstein, *Positive Magic,* 32, 35–54.

[69]Bonewits, *Real Magic,* 117, emphasis in original.

[70]Leek, *Complete Art of Witchcraft,* 64.

[71]See, e.g., Cunningham, *Truth About Witchcraft,* 15, 102, 105, 111, 163; Amber K., "Beginning True Magick," in Kelly, *Neo-Pagan Witchcraft I,* 252; Valiente, *Witchcraft for Tomorrow,* 72–73.

[72]Amber K., "Beginning of True Magick," 252. See also n. 71.

   d. Thus, magic is not connected with the devil, demons, or other evil spirits as uninformed people, like Christians, have believed.

5. Some neo-pagans argue that magic is taught or approved of by the Bible and/or Jesus.

   a. Some neo-pagans argue that magic and other occultic practices are taught or approved of in the Bible.[73]

   b. For example, regarding witchcraft, the witches Gavin and Yvonne Frost contend, "All of the things that you will be taught to do are approved in the Bible in I Corinthians 12."[74]

   c. Some neo-pagans believe that Christ practiced magic and taught occultic doctrines (see II.B.3–4 above).[75]

C. Refutation of Arguments Used by Neo-Pagans to Support Their Positions on Magic/Sorcery[76]

1. Numerous biblical passages reject the practice of magic/sorcery.

   a. The Bible condemns magic. The passages demonstrating such are too numerous to list.[77]

   b. The practice of magic/sorcery is denounced in numerous Old Testament passages (e.g., Ex. 22:18; Deut. 18:10–12; 2 Chron. 33:6; Mal. 3:5). The word used in the above passages (the Hebrew verb *kāshap*) means to enchant, practice magic or sorcery, or use witchcraft.[78]

   c. Contingent upon the context and grammar, *kāshap* can also be translated as "sorcerer(s)" (e.g., Ex. 7:11; Mal. 3:5). The masculine form (*mᵉkashshep*) occurs in Deuteronomy 18:10.

   d. In Exodus 22:18 the feminine form of *kāshap* (*mᵉkashshepâ*) is found. The NIV correctly translates Exodus 22:18: "Do not allow a

---

[73]See, e.g., Cabot and Cowan, *Power of the Witch,* 199, 200, 295; Farrar, *What Witches Do,* 40; Farrar and Farrar, *Witches Bible Compleat,* 2:179; Frost and Frost, *Magic Power of Witchcraft,* 5, 130; Justine Glass, *Witchcraft, The Sixth Sense* (North Hollywood, Calif.: Wilshire Book Co., 1974), 50. For a more extensive treatment of these varied arguments, see my *Witchcraft,* chap. 6.

[74]Frost and Frost, *Magic Power of Witchcraft,* 5; see also 130.

[75]See, e.g., Crowther and Crowther, *Secrets of Ancient Witchcraft,* 164; Farrar and Farrar, *Witches Bible Compleat,* 2:115–16, 136, 177–78, 302, 311; Valiente, *ABC of Witchcraft,* 14.

[76]For a more lengthy biblical critique of occultism, particularly in light of the original languages, see my book *Witchcraft,* chaps. 5 and 6. This treatment is helpful in addressing the arguments of neo-pagans and other occultists who try to circumvent the biblical teaching by the original languages or say that the text was tampered with by the church.

[77]See, e.g., Lev. 19:26, 31; 20:6; 2 Kings 17:16–17; 2 Chron. 33:6; Isa. 8:19–20; 47:9–15; Mal. 3:5; Acts 13:6–11; Gal. 5:19–21; Rev. 9:21; 21:8; 22:15. Some of these passages are discussed in the following points.

[78]Gesenius, Friedrich Heinrich Wilhelm, *A Hebrew and English Lexicon of the Old Testament* (hereafter BDB), ed. Francis Brown, S. R. Driver, and Charles A. Briggs, trans. Edward Robinson (Oxford: Clarendon Press, 1957), 506; *The New International Dictionary of New Testament Theology* (hereafter DNTT), ed. Colin Brown (Grand Rapids: Zondervan, 1976, 1980), vol. 2, s.v. "Magic, Sorcery, Magi"; *The International Standard Bible Encyclopedia* (hereafter ISBE), rev. ed., Geoffrey W. Bromiley (Grand Rapids: Eerdmans, 1986), vol. 3, s.v. "Magic; Magician"; *The New Bible Dictionary* (hereafter NBD), ed. J. D. Douglas (Grand Rapids: Eerdmans, 1962, 1978), s.v. "Magic and Sorcery"; *Theological Wordbook of the Old Testament* (hereafter TWOT), ed. R. Laird Harris (Chicago: Moody, 1980), vol. 1, s.v. 1051.

sorceress to live." The prescribed penalty was death for those who violated God's command.

e. In 2 Kings 9:22; Isaiah 47:9, 12; and Nahum 3:4 sorcery is strongly denounced. The Hebrew word that occurs in these passages is a general term for sorcery, *keshep*, which means magic, magical art, sorcery or sorceries, soothsayer, spell, or witchcraft.[79] Since it occurs only in the plural, it is rightly translated as "sorceries" or "witchcraft(s)."

f. Magic/sorcery is also denounced in the New Testament. In Galatians 5:20 and Revelation 9:21 and 18:23, magic/sorcery is clearly condemned. The Greek word in these passages is *pharmakeia* and means magic or sorcery, or magic arts or sorceries in the plural (as in Rev. 9:21).[80] Galatians 5:21 says, "I warn you . . . that those who live like this will not inherit the kingdom of God."

2. Deuteronomy 18:10–12 is a particularly important text that demonstrates God's disapproval of magic/sorcery.

a. Deuteronomy 18:10–12 definitively declares: "Let no one be found among you who sacrifices his son or daughter in the fire, who practices divination or sorcery, interprets omens, engages in witchcraft, or casts spells, or who is a medium or spiritist or who consults the dead. Anyone who does these things is detestable to the LORD."

b. People who practice magic are equated with those who sacrifice their own children to false gods/goddesses.

c. Spell casting—verse 11

(1) Casting of spells is explicitly forbidden and condemned by God.

(2) The Hebrew word for the phrase in the NIV "casts spells" carries the idea of "casting a spell or tying up a person by magic."[81] The practice itself and those who do it are denounced.

(3) In the prophecy heralding Babylon's judgment from God for its many transgressions—the Babylonians are denounced for performing magical spells (Isa. 47:9, 12).

(4) God's condemnation of the Babylonians for casting spells is a sober warning today to those involved in this form of sorcery.

3. God disapproves not only of the magical practices, but also of those who engage in them.

a. The words used in the Bible for magician(s), sorcerer(s), and sorceress(es) apply across-the-board to those (e.g., neo-pagans) who practice any type of magic/sorcery.

---

[79]BDB, 506; DNTT, vol. 2, s.v. "Magic, Sorcery, Magi"; ISBE, vol. 3, s.v. "Magic; Magician"; TWOT, vol. 1, s.v. 1051a.

[80]BAG, 861.

[81]TWOT, vol. 1, s.v. 598.

b. In the Old Testament, God condemned those who practiced magic/sorcery.

(1) Magicians in the Old Testament are seen only on the wrong side of God's will—flouting his commands and opposing his purposes (e.g., Ex. 7:11, 22; 8:7, 18–19; 9:11).

(2) In Jeremiah 27:9, the Hebrew word *kāshap* occurs. These sorcerers are associated with liars, false prophets, and mediums.

(3) Sorceresses are under the same condemnation and judgment as their male counterparts (see 1.d above).

c. In the New Testament, magicians and sorcerers receive the same rebukes.

(1) As in the Old Testament, these occultists in the New are found trying to oppose God's purposes (see Acts 13:6–12).

(2) Revelation 21:8 gives a radical denunciation—indeed, the eternal judgment—of "those who practice magic arts," or magicians or sorcerers, and the type of individuals associated with them.

(3) Revelation 22:15 tells who will and will not be permitted into the heavenly city: "Outside are the dogs, those who practice magic arts, the sexually immoral, the murderers, the idolaters and everyone who loves and practices falsehood."

(4) The phrase "those who practice magic arts" (NIV) or the word "sorcerers" (NASB) in Revelation 21:8 and 22:15 both correctly translate the Greek word *pharmakos*. Here *pharmakos* means magician or sorcerer—someone who practices magic arts.[82]

4. The power behind magic/sorcery is demonic.

a. Ultimately magic/sorcery (paganism in general) is devised and energized by the devil, the demonic, and our depraved natures (Deut. 32:16–17; Ps. 106:36–39; 1 Cor. 10:20–21; Rev. 9:20–21).

b. Thus, neo-pagans are dealing with the devil and the demonic, despite what they believe or think is possible (John 8:43–44; 2 Cor. 4:3–4; 11:13–14; Eph. 2:2; 4:18; 6:12).[83]

c. Thus, involvement in magic/sorcery (or other forms of occultism or paganism) is spiritual prostitution against the only true God (Ex. 34:16; Lev. 17:7; 20:6; Deut. 32:15–21; Ps. 106:36–39; Jer. 2:1–29; Ezek. 16).

---

[82]BAG, 862; DNTT, s.v. "Magic, Sorcery, Magi"; ISBE, vol. 3, s.v. "Magic; Magician"; NBD, s.v. "Magic and Sorcery."

[83]See DNTT, vol. 1, s.v. "Demon, Air, Cast Out"; and *Theological Dictionary of the New Testament* (hereafter TDNT), ed. Gerhard Kittel and Gerhard Friedrich, trans. and ed. Geoffrey W. Bromiley (Grand Rapids: Eerdmans, 1964), 2:1–20.

D. Arguments Used to Prove the Biblical Doctrine on Magic/Sorcery

1. The Sovereignty of God

   a. God is the sovereign ruler of the universe (III.D.2.b above). His will and purposes prevail in all matters. We cannot manipulate, force, or change his decrees or will. His counsel alone prevails (2 Chron. 20:6; Prov. 16:4, 9; 21:30; Isa. 14:27; Lam. 3:37; Dan. 4:35).

   b. Even when we think we are doing only what we want or wish, we still accomplish God's will (Gen. 50:19–20; 2 Sam. 17:14; Prov. 16:9; 21:1; Isa. 44:28; Acts 4:27–28).

   c. No magic/sorcery can thwart the purposes of God (Ex. 8:16–19; 9:8–11; Isa. 43:13b; 47:9, 11–15; Acts 13:6–12). God cannot be deterred or manipulated by magic/sorcery or any alleged power.

   d. God alone is able to turn "all things" in life, no matter what the circumstances or hardships, for the good of his people (Rom. 8:28).

2. The Privilege of Prayer

   a. The proper source of all blessings—all our needs—is God. God, in part, meets our needs through prayer.

   b. Christians have the privilege of prayer (Luke 18:1; John 14:13–14; 15:7–8; 16:23–24).

   c. God answers the prayers of his people according to his will (Ex. 3:7; Ps. 91:15; Isa. 58:9; Phil. 4:6–7, 19; 1 John 5:14–15).

   d. Prayer is not magic or manipulation.

      (1) Unlike magic, which is forbidden by God, we are told to pray.

      (2) If our requests are in harmony with God's will, they are effectual, because God, the sovereign ruler of the universe, has promised to honor these requests.

      (3) We do not and cannot change God's mind or will through prayer (Num. 23:19; 1 Sam. 15:29), but rather our mind, will, or purposes are brought into line with his.

      (4) Prayer does not require either simple or elaborate rituals, "special" words, or "religious" paraphernalia to be effective. It is done simply in the name of Jesus. Through Jesus, God hears the simplest and humblest of prayers.

      (5) Unlike magic, prayer to God brings a blessing from him.

3. Magic/Sorcery Unnecessary for the Christian

   a. God has already given us everything we need relative to our spiritual well-being (John 10:9–10; 2 Cor. 9:8; Phil. 4:19).

   b. God has given us all we need for life (2 Tim. 3:12–17; 2 Peter 1:3–4). The occult has nothing to offer (John 8:44; Rev. 2:24).

   c. God has promised to give us all the counsel, guidance, or wisdom we will ever need (Col. 2:2–3; James 1:5).

d. God has told us that "the secret things belong to the LORD our God, but the things revealed belong to us and to our children forever, that we may follow all the words of this law" (Deut. 29:29). These are already revealed in the Bible.

VI. The Doctrine of Sin

A. *Neo-Pagan Positions on Sin Briefly Stated*[84]

1. Sin, as defined by orthodox (i.e., biblical) Christianity, does not exist.

2. "Sin"—in the sense of being bad—exists only when one is unbalanced or out of harmony with or estranged from oneself, others, other life-forms, mother earth, the god/dess, the Divine Being, etc.

3. The concept of sin is not beneficial.

B. *Arguments Neo-Pagans Use to Support Their Positions on Sin*

1. Sin, as defined by orthodox (biblical) Christianity, does not exist.

   a. Paul Suliin says: "We have no concept of sin, no score card, in the way Christians understand. We have no concept of salvation, although it's certainly possible to do something wrong."[85]

   b. Adler asserts, "While one can at times be cut off from experiencing the deep and ever-present connection between oneself and the universe, there is no such thing as sin (unless it is simply defined as that estrangement) and guilt is never very useful."[86]

2. "Sin"—in the sense of being bad—exists only when one is unbalanced or out of harmony with or estranged from oneself, others, other life-forms, mother earth, the god/dess, the Divine Being, etc.[87]

   a. An example of "sin" in this sense would include needlessly harming other creatures, polluting mother earth, harming nature, or otherwise not being in tune with nature (see Part I, Sections II.E.1, 3).

   b. Sybil Leek comments: "We permit ourselves to indulge in everything that we wish to do but we do not do anything to excess. So if I wish to drink, smoke, eat caviar, and have a lover there is no law that forbids me to do it on religious grounds, and there is no question of sin, but I am expected to have my pleasures in harmony with other areas of my life."[88]

---

[84]See, e.g., Adler, *Drawing Down the Moon,* ix, 23; Farrar, *What Witches Do,* 49; Leek, *Complete Art of Witchcraft,* 28–29, 52–53, 57–58, 195; Starhawk, *Spiral Dance,* 11, 78.

[85]"Witches lack concept of Sin, but vow to harm no one" (*Press-Telegram* [A.M./P.M.], Long Beach, Calif., 10 January 1990, B3).

[86]Adler, *Drawing Down the Moon,* ix.

[87]See n. 83.

[88]Leek, *Complete Art of Witchcraft,* 52.

57

    c. Examples of "sin" in this sense include interfering with other people's karma or trying to manipulate them or control their lives.

    d. This would also include failing to recognize the actual or potential divinity in people (see Part I, Section II.E.3) or failing to realize and experience the oneness and interconnectedness of all.

    e. This "sin" would also include going against one's own conscience (see Part I, Section II.E.2)—not just doing something one feels he or she shouldn't have, but also not doing something one feels is right because of pressure from others who disagree.

3. The concept of sin is not beneficial.[89]

    a. The concept of sin as defined by Christians and others is seen as not beneficial to individuals or to society.

    b. Sin is often seen as a tool used to control, exploit, or manipulate people—to deprive people of their creativity, freedom, and rights.

    c. Sin only produces anxiety, false guilt, frustration, and neurotic or otherwise unhealthy behavior. In short, it is a false concept.

    d. Also, the notion of sin will not facilitate one's spiritual development or evolution (e.g., realizing one's actual or potential divinity).

C. Refutation of Arguments Used by Neo-Pagans to Support Their Positions on Sin

1. Sin, as defined by orthodox (biblical) Christianity, does exist.

2. Excluding Jesus, all humans are sinners.

    a. Jesus was without sin (John 8:46; Heb. 4:15).

    b. All humans other than Jesus are sinners (2 Chron. 6:36; Ps. 14:1–3; Eccl. 7:20; Isa. 64:6; Rom. 3:9–20, 23; Eph. 2:1–3; 1 John 1:8–10).

3. Human beings, since the fall of Adam, are sinful by nature.

    a. All are born with a sinful nature—in sin or sinful, thus, with a pro-clivity toward sin (Ps. 51:5; Rom. 5:12, 19).

    b. We do not just "sin," but are sinners by nature. One does not have to teach a child how to lie or be selfish. It comes naturally.

    c. News events reveal the horrible reality of individual and corporate sin(s) and its devastating effects.

4. Because of sin all are born spiritually dead.

    a. See Ephesians 2:1–5; Colossians 2:13.

    b. Because of this sinful state we all are, independent of God's grace, blind to or deceived about our spiritual condition (Jer. 17:9; Eph. 4:18)—our hostility and alienation from God (Isa. 59:2; Rom. 8:7; Col. 1:21) and the resulting behavior that stems from our sinful hearts (Matt. 15:18–20; Mark 7:20–23; Gal. 5:17–21).

---

[89]See n. 84.

    c. Outside of the grace of God through Jesus, this is the condition of all humanity.

5. Sin is not a mere imbalance or estrangement from one another or from nature or from one's alleged divine nature.

    a. Sin is not just humanity's inhumanity to other humans or cruelty to animals, but our rebellion or rejection of God and his holy nature. The former are symptoms of the deeper issue, which is our sin nature stemming from our rebellion against God.

    b. Furthermore, humanity's problem (sin) is much worse than our being out of balance with ourselves or with anything or anyone else; it is our alienation from God (see IX.C.3.a, D.2 below) and guilt of being and acting contrary to his holy nature (Ps. 25:11; Rom. 3:19; James 2:10).

    c. Sin is certainly not our alleged estrangement from our supposed potential or actual divinity (see III.C1–2 and IV.C above).

6. The concept of sin is beneficial.

    a. It is a beneficial concept in the sense that—like a fatal physical illness—it must be promptly and properly diagnosed in order for the person who is suffering from it to be treated and cured.

    b. So it is with the ultimate spiritual and physical malaise—sin (Rom. 3:20; 7:13; Gal. 3:24). Sin must be properly diagnosed for what it really is and be treated by Jesus, the divine physician, so that we might have eternal life.

7. Thus, sin does exist and is the ultimate peril of humanity.

D. Arguments Used to Prove the Biblical Doctrine of Sin

1. Humankind is the crown of God's earthly creation (Pss. 8:5–6; 139:14). Gloriously, we have been given the ultimate honor—being made in the image of God (Gen. 1:26–27; 1 Cor. 11:7; James 3:9).

2. Since the fall we have been radically marred or corrupted by sin.

3. Sin is anything contrary to the holy nature of God, for example, as codified in the Ten Commandments.

    a. Sin is contrary to God's nature (Hab. 1:13; James 1:13).

    b. Sin is an offense against God (Ps. 51:4; Isa. 59:12).

    c. Sin is rebellion against God (1 Sam. 15:23; Isa. 1:2).

    d. Sin is any violation of God's holy law (Josh. 23:16; Dan. 9:11; 1 John 3:4).

4. There are many ways we can sin. The following are some examples:

    a. Worshiping false deities is sin (Josh. 23:7, 16; 2 Kings 17:16).

    b. Occultic practice is sin (Deut. 18:10–12; 2 Kings 17:17; Gal. 5:19–21).

    c. Pride is a sin (Ps. 119:21; Prov. 8:13; 21:4; Isa. 2:11).

    d. Sexual immorality is a sin (1 Cor. 6:9, 18: 10:8; 1 Thess. 4:3–5; Rev. 9:21).

e. Lusting is a sin (Matt. 5:28; 1 Peter 4:3).

f. Self-righteousness is a sin (Luke 16:15; 18:9–14; Rom. 10:3–4).

VII. The Doctrine of Salvation

A. *Neo-Pagan Positions on Salvation Briefly Stated*

1. No one needs to be "saved" in the Christian sense of the term.

2. Neo-pagans believe that they "save" themselves.

3. There is no one path, religion, or way to "salvation."

4. Many neo-pagans believe in some form of reincarnation (see point VIII below).

B. *Arguments Used by Neo-Pagans to Support Their Positions on Salvation*

1. No one needs to be "saved" in the Christian sense of the term.

    a. Since there is no divine retribution in the Christian sense, and since there are no sins as Christians understand sin, there is no need of salvation. There is nothing to be saved from.

    b. Valerie Voigt writes, "We don't have a Devil to blame our mistakes on and we need no Savior to save us from a non-existent Hell."[90]

    c. Starhawk says, "We can open new eyes and see that there is nothing to be saved *from*, no struggle of life *against* the universe, no God outside the world to be feared and obeyed."[91]

2. Neo-pagans believe that they "save" themselves.

    a. Many take the expression "the kingdom of God is within you"[92] to mean that the answers to life and/or "salvation" must come from within oneself.

    b. "Salvation" is realizing balance or harmony with oneself, others, the earth, the god/dess, the Divine Being, etc.[93]

    c. We "save" ourselves through knowledge, enlightenment (e.g., spiritual evolution), and good actions.

    d. People "save" themselves by changing, developing their potentials (e.g., their psychic abilities), growing (e.g., in knowledge), evolving spiritually, recognizing or realizing their divinity or potential divinity, and so forth.

3. There is no one path, religion, or way to "salvation."[94]

---

[90]Valerie Voigt, "Being a Pagan in a 9-to-5 World," in *Witchcraft Today, Book One: The Modern Craft Movement,* ed. Chas S. Clifton (St. Paul: Llewellyn, 1992), 173.

[91]Starhawk, *Spiral Dance,* 14, emphasis in original; see also 25.

[92]See, e.g., Adler, *Drawing Down the Moon,* 454; Farrar and Farrar, *Witches Bible Compleat,* 2:136, 311 (n. 2).

[93]See, e.g., Adler, *Drawing Down the Moon,* ix, 4; Leek, *Complete Art of Witchcraft,* 29, 50, 110.

[94]See, e.g., Adler, *Drawing Down the Moon,* viii, 23–38, 169, 172, 299, 455; Buckland, *Complete Book of Witchcraft,* 99; Crowther and Crowther, *Secrets of Ancient Witchcraft,* 159; Cunningham, *Truth About Witchcraft,* 66–67; Farrar and Farrar, *Witches Bible Compleat,* 1:154; 2:179, 279; Luhrmann, *Persuasions,* 7; Starhawk, *Dreaming,* 22, 37–38; Starhawk, *Spiral Dance,* 188–89.

    a. All sincere, "life-affirming" paths, religions, or ways lead to the goddess/god, or divinity, or "salvation."

    b. Raymond Buckland writes, "They [witches] feel that all should be free to choose the religion that best suits them. It would seem obvious that there can be no one religion for all."[95]

    c. Many neo-pagans believe that all paths, religions, or ways ultimately lead to or say the same thing regarding salvation.[96]

4. Many neo-pagans believe in some form of reincarnation (see point VIII below).

C. *Refutation of Arguments Used by Neo-Pagans to Support Their Positions on Salvation*

   1. All human beings are in need of salvation.

    a. All are sinners (see VI.C); therefore, all need a Savior (Rom. 3:20–24; 6:23, 10:9–13; Eph. 2:1–7; 1 Tim. 4:10; 2 Tim. 1:9–10; Titus 2:13–14; 3:4–7; 1 John 4:14).

    b. No one is perfect, which is what they would have to be to deserve heaven or eternal life (see VI.C).

    c. Divine retribution is in store for those whose sins are not forgiven (see IX.C.3 below).

   2. People cannot save themselves.

    a. To believe that one is divine or potentially so is the exact opposite of salvation (Gen. 3:5).

    b. People cannot save themselves (or earn salvation) by good works, knowledge, or otherwise (Rom. 3:20–28; 5:6; Gal. 2:15–16; 3:10–11; Eph. 2:8–9; 2 Tim. 1:9).

    c. No one can "pay the price" (e.g., by good works) for the penalty for our sins. The penalty for our sins is death: physical and spiritual, temporal and eternal. However, Jesus has paid it for us in full (John 19:30; Col. 2:14).

    d. For neo-pagans to quote part of Luke 17:21—"the kingdom of God is within you"—in support of their beliefs is spurious.

      (1) This usage makes the phrase contradict the immediate context of the passage and the entire tenor of the biblical teachings.

      (2) The Greek word translated "within" is *entos*. In the context of Luke 17:21, *entos* means "among" or "in the midst of," not "within" or "inside."

      (3) Hence, the correct translation of this verse is "the kingdom of God is among you (plural)" or "in the midst of you (plural)." In context, the verse does not support neo-pagan beliefs.

[95]Buckland, *Complete Book of Witchcraft*, 99.
[96]Ibid.; Farrar and Farrar, *Witches Bible Compleat*, 1:154.

(4) In context, the passage is teaching, among other points, that the kingdom of God was among them because Jesus, the King of the universe—was right in their geographical midst. Also, since the followers of Jesus (who comprise the kingdom) were among nonfollowers, the kingdom of God was already among them.

3. Not all paths lead to God or salvation.

   a. In one sense, there are many religions, paths, or ways, but they lead not to life or salvation, but to death (Prov. 16:25).

   b. The "broad road" of neo-paganism (i.e., that all sincere "life-affirming" religions are viable) leads not to life or salvation, but to destruction (Matt. 7:13–14).

   c. Sincerity of convictions has nothing to do with the truth or falsity of one's path or way (Prov. 14:12).

   d. There is only one path that leads to salvation (John 14:6; Acts 4:12). Salvation is found only through faith in Jesus Christ (Rom. 10:9–13). All other paths (see Matt. 7) lead to death (Gal. 1:6–9).

   e. Only spuriously could one conclude that all religions teach that we arrive at the same end or goal or believe the same thing.[97]

4. Reincarnation is false (see point VIII below).

D. Arguments Used to Prove the Biblical Doctrine of Salvation

Following are some of the many benefits for those who have appropriated Jesus' atoning, sacrificial, substitutionary work on the cross.

1. God has done for us what we could not do for ourselves—save us from our sins (Rom. 5:6; Eph. 2:1). God has graciously saved us from ourselves.

   a. He has paid in full the penalty for our sins (John 19:30; Col. 2:14).

   b. He has redeemed us from our slavery to sin (John 8:34–36; Rom. 6:6–7, 16–22).

   c. He has set us free from enslavement to the devil (John 8:44–47; 12:31; 16:11; Heb. 2:14; 1 John 3:8).

   d. He has freed us from the fear and power of death (1 Cor. 15:26, 54–57; 2 Tim. 1:10; Heb. 2:15).

   e. He has declared us righteous or justified (Rom. 5:2, 9; Titus 3:7).

2. God's work of salvation puts those who have it applied to them into a right relationship with him.

   a. Moreover, we have been reconciled to God, ending our alienation from him (Rom. 5:10–11; 2 Cor. 5:18–21; Col. 1:21–22).

   b. We have peace with God and with one another only through Jesus (Rom. 5:1).

   c. We have been adopted as God's children (1 John 3:1; 5:19).

---

[97]For a comparison of Christianity with cults and other religions, see George A. Mather and Larry Nichols, *Dictionary of Cults, Sects, Religions and the Occult* (Grand Rapids: Zondervan, 1993).

d. Among other reasons we have been saved is to have a personal relationship and fellowship with God (2 Cor. 13:14; 1 John 1:1–3).

3. The results of God's work of salvation have immediate and eternal benefits for us.

a. We have been rescued from the righteous wrath of God (see IX.C.2.c—IX.C.3.a–e below).

b. Thus, we are no longer under God's righteous condemnation or wrath, but have passed from death to life (John 3:16, 18, 36). We presently possess eternal life (1 John 5:11–13).

c. God has given us "life, and that . . . more abundantly" (John 10:10 KJV) here and now and for all eternity through salvation in Jesus (see IX.D below).

d. God has graciously saved us from ourselves· from death and destruction to a lavish and glorious inheritance in Christ Jesus (Gal. 1:3–4; Eph. 1:3–8; Col. 1:12).

e. All this is the free gift of God (Rom. 6:23) to us through Jesus because of his grace and mercy (Eph. 2:8; 2 Tim. 1:9; Titus 3:4–5).

VIII. The Doctrine of Reincarnation

A. *Neo-Pagan Positions on Reincarnation Briefly Stated*

Many neo-pagans hold to some form of reincarnation.[98]

1. Reincarnation fits with the cyclical nature of life.
2. Rebirths or incarnations are desirable.
3. Reincarnation is necessary to facilitate one's spiritual evolution.
4. Reincarnation provides the answer to life's inequities.
5. Reincarnation was originally taught among Christians.

B. *Arguments Used by Neo-Pagans to Support Their Positions on Reincarnation*

1. Reincarnation fits with the cyclical nature of life.

a. Life is cyclical. Life, death, and rebirth follow each other in endless succession. They are inextricably intertwined. Each is necessary for and dependent on the other, each a vital component or

---

[98]See, e.g., Adler, *Drawing Down the Moon*, 112, 168; Buckland, *Complete Book of Witchcraft*, 17–19; Cabot and Cowan, *Power of the Witch*, 281; Crowther and Crowther, *Secrets of Ancient Witchcraft*, 138; Cunningham, *Truth About Witchcraft*, 62, 65–66; Farrar and Farrar, *Witches Bible Compleat*, 1:154; 2:115–34; Rosemary Ellen Guiley, *The Encyclopedia of Witches and Witchcraft*, (New York: Facts on File, 1989), s.v. "reincarnation"; Kelly, *Neo-Pagan Witchcraft I*, introduction; Leek, *Complete Art of Witchcraft*, 28, 138–51; Sybil Leek, *Reincarnation: The Second Chance* (New York: Bantam Books, 1975), *passim*; Roberts, *Witches, U.S.A.*, 21–22, 143, 147–49; Ceisiwr Serith, *The Pagan Family: Handing the Old Ways Down* (St. Paul: Llewellyn, 1994), 197–99; Starhawk, *Spiral Dance*, 84, 98; Valiente, *ABC of Witchcraft*, 14, 322–26; Weinstein, *Positive Magic*, 97–125.

link to the complete process or cycle of life. Death—as well as rebirth—is part of this process of the entire cycle of life.

b. Starhawk says: "The secret of immortality lies in seeing death as an integral part of the cycle of life. Nothing is ever lost from the universe: Rebirth can be seen in life itself, where every ending brings a new beginning. Most witches do believe in some form of reincarnation."[99]

2. Rebirths or incarnations are desirable.

a. Many neo-pagans see reincarnation as a blessing, not as a curse or something to avoid.

b. Kelly comments: "Most Witches believe that human beings do not necessarily have immortal souls. The Craft promises 'rebirth among those you love' as the reward of the true initiates (the complete opposite of Eastern concepts)."[100]

c. Starhawk declares: "Rebirth is not considered to be condemnation to an endless, dreary round of suffering, as in Eastern religions. Instead, it is seen as the great gift of the Goddess."[101]

3. Reincarnation is necessary to facilitate one's spiritual evolution.

a. For many neo-pagans, reincarnation is necessary for one's spiritual evolution or growth.[102]

b. The neo-pagan Ceisiwr Serith says: "There are two theories of how the circumstances of rebirth are determined. One is that the soul itself decides, based on what it feels it most needs to continue its advancement towards godhood."[103]

c. One aspect of spiritual evolution is a person's need to encounter the full range of possible experiences.

(1) Raymond Buckland declares: "Why should one person be born into a rich family and another into poverty? . . . if not because we must all eventually experience all things."[104]

(2) In regard to an interview, Sybil Leek reported: "My moderator friend asked me if I felt I had to experience being a murderer. I certainly do not in this life, because I know I have evolved beyond the idea of taking life. . . . Probably in one of my past lives, I too was a murderer; if this is so, then I also accept that in another incarnation I could have been a victim. If we accept logic, we must accept it on all issues."[105]

---

[99]Starhawk, *Spiral Dance*, 84.

[100]Kelly, *Neo-Pagan Witchcraft I*, introduction.

[101]Starhawk, *Spiral Dance*, 27.

[102]See Buckland, *Complete Book of Witchcraft*, 17.

[103]Serith, *Pagan Family*, 198. The other theory is that a person is reincarnated according to one's karma, not according to one's own choice.

[104]Buckland, *Complete Book of Witchcraft*, 17, ellipsis in the original.

[105]Leek, *Complete Art of Witchcraft*, 147.

4. Reincarnation provides the answer to life's inequities.

    a. Many neo-pagans also believe that reincarnation explains the seeming injustices, unfairness, or inequalities of life.

    b. Relative to reincarnation and hardships Roberts writes: "Therefore, your life is your responsibility alone. If your mother was a fool and your father a brute, that's their misfortune, not yours. Nor does it matter how brutal or hopeless such circumstances may seem. If they are physically or emotionally insurmountable, then you are merely discharging a debt which you incurred through misusing some of the assets you enjoyed in a previous life."[106]

    c. Thus, whether for good or for ill, one's present circumstances are related to reincarnation.

5. Reincarnation was originally taught in the Bible and among Christians.[107] Leek states, "In 551 A.D. the Christian religion officially detached itself from belief in reincarnation."[108]

C. Refutation of Arguments Used by Neo-Pagans to Support Their Positions on Reincarnation

1. Death is our enemy, not a necessary or desirable link in the chain or process of life (see IX.C.1 below).

2. Reincarnation does not have the answers to the injustices and disparities of life. It only generates more difficulties, more questions.[109]

    a. The theory of reincarnation as advanced by probably all neo-pagans justifies any action or state of affairs—including catastrophic, evil, and immoral ones. It not only sanctions evil events, but actually mandates that they ought to happen. That is, bad things must happen for our own good.

    b. For example:[110]

        (1) Susan Roberts writes: "You even chose the circumstances of your birth in order to gain a particular life experience which will speed your progression to an ever-ascending higher plane as one life succeeds another. Therefore, your life is your responsibility alone. . . . Nor does it matter how brutal or hopeless such circumstances may seem. If they are physically or

---

[106]Roberts, *Witches, U.S.A.*, 149.

[107]See, e.g., Buckland, *Complete Book of Witchcraft*, 235; Leek, *Complete Art of Witchcraft*, 156; Valiente, *ABC of Witchcraft*, 322.

[108]Leek, *Complete Art of Witchcraft*, 156.

[109]Because of space, we can only highlight the ethical difficulties that reincarnation itself generates. For more thorough treatments, see Norman L. Geisler and J. Yutaka Amano, *The Reincarnation Sensation* (Wheaton, Ill.: Tyndale, 1986); and Albrecht, *Reincarnation: A Christian Critique of a New Age Doctrine*.

[110]Many other quotes could be produced to demonstrate the same point. See Buckland, *Complete Book of Witchcraft*, 17–18; Cabot and Cowan, *Power of the Witch*, 202, 221, 280–82; Leek, *Complete Art of Witchcraft*, 32, 47, 146–47; Leek, *Reincarnation*, 41, 45–50; Roberts, *Witches, U.S.A.*, 147–50; Starhawk, *Spiral Dance*, 27–30, 99; Weinstein, *Positive Magic*, 98–100, 102–4, 110–11, 114, 249–50.

emotionally insurmountable, then you are merely discharging a debt you incurred through misusing some of the assets you enjoyed in a previous life."[111]

(2) Weinstein writes: "Within the karmic frame of reference, there are no accidents or coincidences. Nobody does anything to us unless we let them (or invite them)."[112]

c. From these examples we see:

(1) In some sense, for many neo-pagans, *we* are responsible for almost everything, if not everything, that happens to us in life.

(2) It is for our own good—our spiritual growth or evolution.

d. Thus, most or all of whatever occurs ought to happen. This line of reasoning is an instance of the "naturalistic fallacy."

(1) This fallacy occurs when one assumes that whatever exists *ought to* exist.

(2) Weinstein is representative in confounding the two: "We may judge not only ourselves as 'bad' (if we perceive error or negative behavior) but also judge Dark or negative aspects anywhere in life, as 'bad' (i.e., death is bad, illness is bad, weakness is bad, old age is bad, anger, anxiety, worry, fear, insecurity, mistakes—all these and many other common occurrences may seem 'bad'). But this is like saying the moon is bad when it wanes to crescent form, or that the sun is bad on a cloudy day. *There is no judgment on the Dark.*"[113]

(3) But just because a situation happens, it does not follow that it ought to. By this faulty reasoning it follows, for example, that since racism exists, therefore it ought (morally) to exist.

(4) Because of this fatal flaw in thinking and moral reasoning, the most heinous atrocities can be justified (such as the Holocaust). Logically, this leads to moral apathy and even a form of fatalism.

3. Reincarnation was not taught by Jesus, the Bible, or the early church.

a. There is no objective evidence that Jesus ever taught any form of reincarnation.[114]

b. Jesus was a monotheistic Jew (Deut. 6:4–5; Mark 12:28–32) who held to the entire teachings of the Old Testament (Matt. 5:17–19). Reincarnation as a worldview is the complete opposite of the biblical worldview Jesus accepted and taught. They are mutually exclusive (see point D below).

---

[111]Roberts, *Witches, U.S.A.,* 149.

[112]Weinstein, *Positive Magic,* 98; see also 103.

[113]Ibid., 250, emphasis in original.

[114]For solid treatments on this, see Albrecht, *Reincarnation,* and Geisler and Amano, *Reincarnation Sensation.* See also Ron Rhodes' volume *New Age Movement* in this series; or Doug Groothuis, *Revealing the New Age Jesus* (Downers Grove, Ill.: InterVarsity Press, 1990).

    c. There is no objective evidence that the early church ever taught reincarnation.[115] Once again, occultists try to import teachings into the church.

    d. Nor was reincarnation once taught in the Bible but later expunged.

        (1) Some claim that the Second Council of Constantinople in A.D. 553 removed references to reincarnation from the Bible.[116]

        (2) Historically, the only people who have tampered with the text of the Bible were pagans.[117]

        (3) The existing ancient manuscript evidence for the Old and New Testaments is excellent. We possess thousands of partial and complete manuscripts of the Old and New Testaments.[118]

        (4) A number of extant partial and complete Greek New Testament manuscripts predate the Second Council of Constantinople by one to three centuries. None contain the supposedly expunged passages teaching reincarnation.

    e. The passages that neo-pagans and others point to as teaching reincarnation, in context, do not support their contentions.[119] Occultists are the ones tampering with the Bible.

D. Arguments Used to Prove the Biblical Doctrine Relative to Reincarnation

1. The Bible does not, and never did, teach reincarnation in any form.

2. The biblical doctrine of salvation by grace alone through faith alone in Christ alone contradicts reincarnation.

    a. Unlike reincarnation, the Bible teaches that salvation is the free, unmerited gift of God (Rom. 3:24; 6:23; Eph. 2:8–9).

    b. Unlike reincarnation, the Bible teaches that salvation is not merited by works (Rom. 3:20, 27–28; 4:6; 9:30–32; 11:6; Gal. 2:15–16; 3:10–11; Eph. 2:8–9; 2 Tim. 1:9), but by grace.

    c. God is able to save us based on the finished work of Christ (John 19:30; Rom. 3:21–26; 5:1–11; 6:23; Col. 1:21–23; Titus 3:4–7).

3. Contrary to reincarnation, the Bible teaches that we live only once.

    a. According to Hebrews 9:27, we get only one life on this earth, not multiple lives.

    b. After physical death at the end of a person's one and only life on this present earth, that person goes either to heaven to await the resurrection because of faith in Christ (2 Cor. 5:8; Phil. 1:21–23), or to

---

[115]See Albrecht, *Reincarnation.* See also Robert Bowman, "Reincarnation—Did the Church Suppress It?" *Christian Research Journal* 10, no. 1 (Summer 1987), 8–12.

[116]See Albrecht, *Reincarnation,* and Bowman, "Reincarnation."

[117]See Geisler and Nix, *Introduction to the Bible,* 278–82, 446.

[118]See ibid., particularly chaps. 20, 22–24.

[119]See Albrecht, *Reincarnation;* Bowman, "Reincarnation"; and Geisler and Amano, *Reincarnation Sensation.*

a place of punishment to await the day of God's final judgment (2 Peter 2:9; Rev. 20:11–15).

c. Just as Christ died only once for our sins (Heb. 1:3; 9:25–28; 10:10, 12), so the person who has not trusted in Christ will face only one final judgment. There is no cycle of life, death, judgment, and so on. This one judgment determines one's eternal destiny.

d. There are no other options or second chances after one's physical death.

4. Thus, the biblical position on the afterlife or salvation completely contradicts reincarnation (see VI.C–D; VII.C–D; IX.D).

IX. The Doctrine of Eschatology

A. Neo-Pagan Positions on Eschatology Briefly Stated

1. For many neo-pagans, physical death is not final, nor is it to be feared.[120]

2. After physical death, many hope to arrive at Summerland (or some comparable place), then eventually reincarnate on a physical plane again among those they love (see VIII.B.2.b above).[121]

3. Most neo-pagans believe that hell or any other place of final punishment does not exist.

4. Many neo-pagans attempt to contact spirits (e.g., the dead or other entities). Thus, they are involved in necromancy and divination.

B. Arguments Used by Neo-Pagans to Support Their Positions on Eschatology

1. Death is not final, nor is it to be feared.

a. Many neo-pagans believe that death is natural and necessary to the complete cycle of life: birth, death, rebirth (see VIII.B.1 above).

b. Marion Weinstein writes: "In the occult view, death is neither horrible nor frightening. We believe in the eternal life of the soul, and we work with the concept of contact between the Worlds. The change-over from this physical form may seem mysterious, but it is not final."[122]

c. Starhawk says, "Death is not an end; it is a stage in the cycle that leads on to rebirth."[123]

---

[120]See, e.g., Cabot and Cowan, *Power of the Witch,* 280–82; Farrar and Farrar, *Witches Bible Compleat,* 2:75, 118–20, 326; Neilson and Cavanaugh, "She of Many Names," 122, 123; Serith, *Pagan Family,* 197–200; Starhawk, *Dreaming,* 40; Starhawk, *Spiral Dance,* 27, 78, 80–81, 84, 98–99; Weinstein, *Positive Magic,* 102–4, 249–50.

[121]See, e.g., Crowther and Crowther, *Secrets of Ancient Witchcraft,* 138; Guiley, *Encyclopedia of Witches,* s.v. "reincarnation"; Serith, *Pagan Family,* 197; Starhawk, *Spiral Dance,* 27.

[122]Weinstein, *Positive Magic,* 104.

[123]Starhawk, *Spiral Dance,* 27.

2. After physical death, many hope to arrive at Summerland, then eventually reincarnate among those they love.

   a. The neo-pagan's Summerland or its counterparts is, in a sense, analogous to Christianity's heaven.

   b. Starhawk says, "After death, the human soul is said to rest in 'Summerland,' the Land of Eternal Youth, where it is refreshed, grows young, and is made ready to be born again."[124]

3. There is no hell or other place of punishment.

   a. Valerie Voigt speaks of hell as "non-existent."[125]

   b. Asked whether witches believe in hell, the Crowthers say, "No. The whole idea of burning forever in a blazing pit is very farfetched, and certainly doesn't tie up with a god [*sic*] of love. This idea was invented to frighten an uneducated people into being 'good' and going to church."[126]

4. Many neo-pagans attempt to contact spirits (e.g., the dead or other entities). Thus, they are involved in necromancy and divination.

   a. Some attempt to contact the spirits of dead human beings (necromancy).

      (1) Many neo-pagans believe that when people physically die they do not cease to exist, but go to Summerland, the Otherworld, or some other realm of existence and can still be contacted.

      (2) For example, referring to neo-pagans' ancestors, Serith says: "They are mediators between us and the spirit world. . . . They are still interested in us, with one foot in our world and one in the Otherworld. A belief in reincarnation does not mitigate their influence; the Otherworld is all times and all places, and reborn souls can therefore still be contacted through it."[127]

      (3) Doreen Valiente declares, "One of the objects of present-day witches' rites is to contact the spirits of those who have been witches in their past lives on earth."[128]

   b. Some contact other entities.

      (1) Ceisiwr Serith tells people how to invite various spirits or guardian spirits into their homes and lives.[129]

      (2) Even the druid Isaac Bonewits, a materialist magician, believes that people can in a sense contact "spirits" or entities.[130]

---

[124]Starhawk, *Spiral Dance*, 27.

[125]Voigt, "Being a Pagan in a 9-to-5 World," 173.

[126]Crowther and Crowther, *Secrets of Ancient Witchcraft*, 161.

[127]Serith, *Pagan Family*, 24. See also 4, 28.

[128]Valiente, *ABC of Witchcraft*, 157.

[129]Serith, *Pagan Family*, 3–5, 19–35, 43–44.

[130]Bonewits, *Real Magic*, 41–42, 133–34, 137–38, 145, 157, 158, 218, 220.

      (3) Laurie Cabot says, "I always encourage children to have dreams . . . in which they will meet their spirit guides or animal helpers."[131]

   c. Some neo-pagans practice divination through contacting these entities.

      (1) When necromancy or other forms of spiritism are done to obtain information, they are also a form of divination.

      (2) Imogen Cavanagh says of Samhain (Halloween), that "it is a night for divination too"[132] because of spirits roaming around.

      (3) Doreen Valiente attests regarding witchcraft, "Divination in all its forms has always been an important part of the witch's craft."[133]

      (4) Valiente also avows: "It is notable that Spiritualist mediums of the present day claim to be aided by spirits whom they call 'Guides'; that is, spirits who particularly attach themselves to a medium for the purpose of assisting in . . . advising the medium. Without wishing in any way to give offence to Spiritualists, this is exactly what the human familiar of the witches did and still does."[134]

      (5) Of the family shrine and the guardian(s) or spirit(s) that accompany it, Serith says, "Your guardians can give advice and help if you take the time to honor them and ask for it."[135]

C. *Refutation of Arguments Used by Neo-Pagans to Support Their Positions on Eschatology*

  1. Death is not natural, nor our friend, nor simply necessary to complete the process of life.

    a. There is no "cycle of life" in the sense of birth, death, rebirth, etc.

    b. To say that death is merely natural or necessary is the naturalistic fallacy: assuming that whatever is ought to be.[136]

    c. Death is our last enemy (1 Cor. 15:26, 54–57; Heb. 2:14).

    d. Death exists only because of sin.

  2. Summerland does not exist.

    a. There are only two places people go to after their physical death: heaven or hell (see VII.C.3 above). Thus, there is no Summerland.

      (1) There are numerous differences between the neo-pagan Summerland and the biblical heaven.

---

[131]Cabot and Cowan, *Power of the Witch,* 278.
[132]Neilson and Cavanagh, "She of Many Names," 123.
[133]Valiente, *ABC of Witches,* 117.
[134]Ibid.
[135]Serith, *Pagan Family,* 31.
[136]See Section VIII.C.2.d above.

      (2) Those in heaven will receive an incorruptible, glorified, resurrected physical body for eternity (1 Cor. 15:51–54; Phil. 3:20–21), while those in Summerland will eventually be reincarnated into a new corruptible physical body, even myriad times.

      (3) There will be no sin or imperfection in heaven, whereas people in Summerland are still imperfect beings.

  b. Those who have trusted in Jesus Christ as their personal Lord and Savior go to be with him (2 Cor. 5:8; Phil. 1:21–23).

  c. Those who have *not* trusted in Jesus Christ as their personal Lord and Savior go to the place of punishment (Matt. 25:41, 46; 2 Thess. 1:8–9; 2 Peter 2:9; Rev. 20:11–15; see next point).

3. The Bible teaches the reality of hell.

  a. Sin results in separation or alienation from God (Ps. 5:4–6; Isa. 59:1–2; 64:5–7; Mic. 3:4; Eph. 2:12; 4:18; Col. 1:21).

  b. The ultimate effect of sin is death (Gen. 2:17; Rom. 6:23; James 1:15), both physical (Gen. 2:17; 3:19; Ezek. 18:4, 20; Rom. 5:12–17) and spiritual (Rom. 7:11; Eph. 2:1–5; Col. 2:13). The final result of spiritual death is eternal separation from God.

  c. Because of our sin, without the saving work of Jesus, all are under the condemnation of God (John 3:18) and destined to eternal separation and punishment from God.

  d. The result or "reward" of sin is eternal judgment and punishment (Dan. 12:2; Matt. 18:8; 25:31–46; 2 Thess. 1:9; Rev. 20:10–15).

  e. The sentence is final, eternal. There is no second chance.

4. The Bible condemns spiritism, necromancy, and divination in all forms.

  a. Spiritism

      (1) Spiritism is expressly forbidden and condemned in the Bible (Lev. 19:31; 20:6, 27; Deut. 18:10–12; 2 Kings 21:6; 23:24; 2 Chron. 33:6; Isa. 8:19).

      (2) Deuteronomy 18:10–12 definitively declares: "Let no one be found among you who sacrifices his son or daughter in the fire, who practices divination or sorcery, interprets omens, engages in witchcraft, or casts spells, or who is a medium or spiritist or who consults the dead. Anyone who does these things is detestable to the LORD."

      (3) The word translated "spiritist" in the NIV is the Hebrew *yidd^e'ōnî*. It is sometimes translated "familiar spirit," "soothsayer," or "wizard" (KJV). Among its meanings is "a knowing one"; someone supposedly familiar with secrets of the spirit world, a spiritist, soothsayer, or wizard.[137] Thus, a spiritist is an adept of the occult.

---

[137]BDB, 396; DNTT, vol. 2, s.v. "Magic, Sorcery, Magi"; ISBE, vol. 3, s.v. "Medium"; TWOT, vol. 1, s.v. "848d."

(4) Involvement in spiritism is to interact or consort with demonic spirits (Deut. 32:17; Ps. 106:37–39), hence is expressly condemned.

b. Necromancy

(1) Necromancy is clearly forbidden and condemned in the Bible (Deut. 18:10–12; 1 Sam. 28:7–8; 1 Chron. 10:13–14; Isa. 8:19).

(2) This form of spiritism and/or divination is impermissible.

(3) Thus, neo-pagans who engage in necromancy fall under the biblical condemnations of those who practice such.

c. Divination (e.g., Mediumship)

(1) Divination is denounced (e.g., Lev. 19:26, 31; 20:6, 27; Deut. 18:10–12, 14; 1 Sam. 15:23; 2 Kings 17:16–17; 21:6; 1 Chron. 10:13–14; 2 Chron. 33:6; Acts 16:16–18). For the sake of space, we will limit discussion to divination relative to spiritism/necromancy (e.g., mediumship or "channeling").

(2) Mediumship (one form at least)—or what is popularly known today as channeling—can be a form of divination.[138]

(3) Mediumship is specifically and explicitly forbidden and condemned in the Bible (e.g., Lev. 19:31; 20:6, 27; Deut. 18:10–12; 2 Kings 21:6; 23:24; 1 Chron. 10:13–14; Acts 16:16–18).

(4) The Hebrew word for medium, *'ôb,* occurs in numerous Old Testament passages (e.g., all those listed in point c). The word can mean a medium; necromancer; someone who contacts, consults, or inquires of "ghosts" or the dead or a familiar spirit(s). The "witch" (KJV) of Endor was an *'ôb*—a medium.[139]

(5) A medium is a person who either is possessed by or otherwise calls up, contacts, interacts, or traffics with "the dead," a familiar spirit(s), or spirit(s).

(6) Acts 16:16–18 relates a case of divination by mediumship. A slave girl possessed by a "spirit of divination" (NASB) could supposedly predict (divine) or foretell the future. The point is that the girl was possessed by a demonic spirit by which she practiced divination.

(7) Those involved in divination of any kind are involved in biblically forbidden practices and with, knowingly or not, the demonic—hence, God's judgment. The penalty for mediums in the Old Testament, as for all other occultists, was death (Deut. 18:10–12; Lev. 19:31; 20:27).

---

[138]It is also a form of spiritism and, in certain cases, of necromancy (e.g., 1 Sam. 28:7–13).

[139]BDB, 15; DNTT, vol. 2, s.v. "Magic, Sorcery, Magi"; ISBE, vol. 1, s.v. "Divination"; ISBE, vol. 3, s.v. "Medium"; TWOT, vol. 1, s.v. "37a."

D. Arguments Used to Prove the Biblical Doctrine of Eschatology

1. Humans are immortal. We will live throughout all eternity. From the point of time that we are conceived, we will live forevermore.

   a. Everyone will be resurrected. There will be a resurrection of the righteous and the unrighteous—those who have saving faith in Christ and those who do not (Dan. 12:2; John 5:25–29; 6:44; 11:24–26; Acts 24:15; Rev. 20:4–6, 13).

   b. Depending on one's relationship with Christ, a person will spend eternity either with God (in heaven) or without him (in hell).

2. Those who reject Jesus Christ as their personal Lord and Savior will be eternally separated from the one true triune God. Those who practice paganism or some other form of occultism will be excluded from God's presence (Gal. 5:19–21; Rev. 20:11–15; 21:8; 22:15).

3. Those who have trusted in Jesus Christ as their personal Lord and Savior will spend eternity in fellowship with the one true triune God.

   a. At death Christians go to be with the Lord and to await the bodily resurrection (Job 19:25–27; Isa. 26:19; 1 Cor. 15:42–44, 51–53; 2 Cor. 5:1–8; Phil. 1:21–23; 3:20–21; 1 Thess. 4:13–17).

   b. Jesus Christ has conquered death (1 Cor. 15:54–57; Heb. 2:14–15). Those who trust in him receive the benefits of his victory (John 3:16–17; John 6:44, 47; 11:25–26; Rom. 6:23; 10:9).

   c. Salvation has been provided for us by God himself (Ex. 15:2; Ps. 62:1; Isa. 12:2; John 3:16–17; Rom. 3:22–26; Eph. 1:3–7).

   d. God freely offers salvation or eternal life through the finished work of Jesus Christ (John 3:16–17; 6:40; 1 John 4:9–19; 5:11–13).

   e. The only way to obtain salvation or to be reconciled to God for eternity is through the finished work of Christ (John 14:6; Acts 4:12). Through him alone is the forgiveness of our sin (Acts 10:43).

   f. Those who have a relationship with the one true and living God through Jesus will spend eternity in fellowship with him (2 Cor. 6:16; 1 John 1:1–3; Rev. 21:3) in the new heaven and new earth (Rev. 21–22). Thus, only those who have trusted in Christ for salvation will escape the righteous wrath of God (1 Thess. 5:9).

Part III: Witnessing Tips

I. Suggested Approaches to Witnessing to Neo-Pagans

A. *Understand a common neo-pagan perspective against proselytizing.*

1. Most neo-pagans do not like to be proselytized.

   a. Since most do not believe that there is any one truth or right religion, there cannot be only one right religion for everybody.

   b. Many think that only bigots or unenlightened and arrogant people think they have the one right religion or truth for everyone.

   c. Most neo-pagans value autonomy, the freedom to believe and do what *they* want.

   d. Thus, the mere fact that you would share with them or try to convert them is often perceived as intolerance or bigotry. Sharing the gospel could be taken as an insult.

2. Be prepared to respond to this perspective.

   a. Understand this perspective, be sensitive to neo-pagans, yet be prepared to show why you want to talk regarding these matters.

   b. Perhaps let them know in advance that you understand this perspective but are willing to risk their disapproval because of the ramifications of these views.

   c. Point out that since they are open-minded people, they ought to be interested in talking with you.

   d. Let them know that you do not want to argue with them but want to civilly and intelligently discuss the issues.

   e. Inform them and remind yourself that love divorced from truth is the worst form of hate. Therefore, we risk rejection in order to share the gospel—the best news.

B. *Ask neo-pagans certain key questions.*

   Be prepared not just to talk but to ask key questions and then listen attentively to the responses.

1. Ask epistemological questions such as the following:[1]

   a. How do you know that neo-paganism is true?

---

[1]Epistemology is the consideration of how and what we can know, and why.

     b. How do you define truth?

     c. How do you know what "things" are true?

     d. How do you know that Christianity is not true?

     e. What would convince you—if anything would—that neo-paganism is not true or that Christianity is true?

2. Ask why they are involved in neo-paganism.

     a. Like a good medical doctor who learns a patient's medical history before giving treatment, discover as much as you possibly can about the other person.

     b. Ask questions such as:

          (1) How, when, and why did you get involved?

          (?) What generated your interest in the first place?

          (3) Why are you still involved?

          (4) What benefit do you derive from it?

          (5) What needs do you feel it meets for you?

          (6) What do you like the most about it?

          (7) What do you like the least about it?

          (8) What are you most uncomfortable with regarding your views and practices?

3. Ask, "What do *you* believe, hold to, or practice?"

     a. Since there is such diversity among neo-pagans, do not assume that you know exactly what the other person believes or does.

     b. For example, do not assume that they perform rituals in the nude.

4. Do not do all the talking; take time to listen and show genuine interest in them.

C. *Show genuine concern.*

1. If you don't have a genuine concern for the individual(s), pray for such from the Lord.

2. See them for who they are—fellow humans made in the image of God, who will spend eternity separated from him.

D. *Be prepared for spiritual warfare.*

1. Witnessing is not merely an intellectual issue, but an emotional and ultimately spiritual one.

     a. The gospel is hidden from people because the "god of this age" has spiritually blinded them (2 Cor. 4:4).

     b. They are blind to the truth of the gospel because they are spiritually dead and involved in sin (Eph. 2:1–5; 4:18–19).

2. Therefore, there is an urgent need for prayer for the individual: before, during, and after sharing.

E. Learn five primary approaches for witnessing to neo-pagans.

1. Biblical Teaching Approach

   a. First, the Christian ought to use the Bible and its teachings as much as possible in dialogue with neo-pagans.

      (1) You don't always have to quote a passage verbatim or cite the exact source.

      (2) But your conversation should be "peppered" with Scripture.

   b. Because neo-pagans generally do not believe in the Bible or only interpret it according to preconceived views, they may not be willing to listen to direct quotes.

   c. Thus, do not be surprised if many neo-pagans are not receptive to this approach or outright hostile to it.

   d. Nonetheless, we should still use the Bible—the Word of God—because it will accomplish what God desires. The Holy Spirit will work through the Bible to accomplish his will (Isa. 55:11; Jer. 23:29; Heb. 4:12; 1 Peter 1:23–25).

2. Historical Reliability of the Bible and Historicity of Jesus Approach

   a. The historical reliability of the Bible

      (1) Be prepared to present some *basic* information to show that the Bible is historically reliable, is not mythological literature, and has not been tampered with by Christians.

      (2) This can be done by moderately familiarizing oneself with the material from any one of the books listed in Part II, nn. 30 and 34, or by consulting John Montgomery, *History and Christianity* (Minneapolis: Bethany House, 1965) or *Where Is History Going?* (Minneapolis: Bethany House, 1972)—pages 49 and 52, for example.

   b. The historicity of Jesus

      (1) From the historically reliable New Testament documents we can confidently study the life of the historical Jesus Christ.

      (2) Based on an honest and thorough investigation of these primary documents, we are convinced of Jesus' historicity and unique claims and proofs of deity (see Part II, Sections II.C.–D.).

      (3) There is solid confirmation for the historicity of Jesus and his claims, as opposed to the mythical figures of neo-paganism.[2]

      (4) For those who are unwilling to consider the historical evidence of the New Testament documents themselves, we can utilize

---

[2]See the works referenced in Part II, n. 30. See also J. Gresham Machen, *The Origin of Paul's Religion* (Grand Rapids: Eerdmans, 1925); Ronald H. Nash, *The Gospel and the Greeks* (Richardson, Tex.: Probe Books, 1992); F. F. Bruce, *The New Testament Documents: Are They Reliable?* 5th rev. ed. (Grand Rapids: Eerdmans, 1960), 119.

external sources (i.e., other than the New Testament) to verify Jesus' existence as well (see Part II, n. 31).

(5) These sources are invaluable for external confirmation of the historical personage of Jesus presented in the New Testament.

3. Tender-Minded Approach

a. This terminology is not used as an insult. It has been used (e.g., by William James) for those who have a strong appreciation for aesthetics and the arts, such as poetry and other forms of literature. For some individuals, this appreciation is more effective than appealing to rigorous research or logical analysis.

b. This is not—at least not at first—a direct or "hard" approach, but utilizes the person's interest, as through literature or stories or fairy tales or myths, to communicate the basic gospel hope and message.

c. Christians such as C. S. Lewis and J. R. R. Tolkien have successfully used this approach.[3] Using this approach, Christians can share the gospel hope with many neo-pagans who have a great love for allegories, fairy tales, myths, and other archetypal literature.[4]

d. This is a different but promising approach for pre-evangelism.

4. Use of Logic Approach

a. The competent and consistent application of logic is devastating to many of the claims of neo-pagans (e.g., that logic does not apply to metaphors or religious concerns).

b. Seek to become proficient in the basics of logic (e.g., the four primary laws of logic) and its usage.[5] This is a harder or more direct approach in witnessing to neo-pagans in that it attempts to undercut the foundations of their views.

(1) Logic should be employed to show the silly and self-stultifying (self-refuting) or contradictory claims and ethical dilemmas that result from many neo-pagan views.[6]

---

[3]For masterful examples of this, see the writings of C. S. Lewis (e.g., *The Chronicles of Narnia, Out of the Silent Planet, Perelandra, That Hideous Strength*) and J. R. R. Tolkien (e.g., *The Lord of the Rings*).

[4]See C. S. Lewis, "Myth Became Fact," in *God in the Dock*, ed. Walter Hooper (Grand Rapids: Eerdmans, 1970); C. S. Lewis, *Surprised by Joy* (San Diego: Harcourt, Brace, Jovanovich, 1956); John W. Montgomery, ed., *Myth, Allegory, and Gospel* (Minneapolis: Bethany Fellowship, 1974); Richard L. Purtill, *J. R. R. Tolkien: Myth, Morality, and Religion* (San Francisco: Harper & Row, 1984); J. R. R. Tolkien, "On Fairy-Stories," in *Essays Presented to Charles Williams* (Grand Rapids: Eerdmans, 1966), by Dorothy Sayers, J. R. R. Tolkien, C. S. Lewis et al.

[5]To become familiar with or to refresh oneself with the basics of logic, see Irving M. Copi, *Introduction to Logic*, 7th ed. (New York: Macmillan, 1986); Norman L. Geisler and Ronald M. Brooks, *Come Let Us Reason* (Grand Rapids: Baker, 1990); Patrick J. Hurley, *A Concise Introduction to Logic*, 5th ed. (Belmont, Calif.: Wadsworth, 1994); or Ronald Nash, *Worldviews in Conflict* (Grand Rapids: Zondervan, 1992), 80–84.

[6]For other examples of self-refuting statements and how to critique them, see Geisler, *Christian Apologetics* (Grand Rapids: Baker, 1976), 141–45; Norman L. Geisler and William D. Watkins, *Worlds Apart: A Handbook on World Views*, 2d ed. (Grand Rapids: Baker, 1989), 262–69; Nash, *Worldviews in Conflict*, 55–57, 80–84.

(2) Self-refuting statements, such as the notion that "all truth is relative," should be shown for what they are—absurd. For example, first, note that all truth is allegedly relative. Second, supposedly the above statement is a truth or they would not have presented it. Third, if it is a truth, then it too is relative. Fourth, if the statement "all truth is relative" is a truth and is therefore relative, then it is not always true that all truth is relative. Fifth, if at least some truths are not relative (e.g., this one), then they would be absolute. Sixth, thus, not all truths are relative and hence some truths are absolute. Seventh, thus the original statement is false, indeed, is self-contradictory.

5. Worldview Critiques Approach

   a. Logic should not only be applied to individual truth claims but to their entire worldview as well.[7]

   b. Many profound problems (philosophical and otherwise) are inherent in the worldviews of polytheism,[8] pantheism,[9] panentheism,[10] or any attempted combination of these views.

   c. None of these views has an adequate or morally acceptable answer to the problem of evil (e.g., in pantheism and panentheism, evil emanates or flows naturally and necessarily from the divinity).

   d. Polytheism, pantheism, and panentheism have other ethical dilemmas, such as how one derives a sense of moral rightness or wrongness or a just ethical standard consistent with these worldviews.

   e. In the best sense, these and other inherent problems should be exploited to show that they are not credible worldviews.

   f. There are also serious problems with reincarnation, which is a significant component of the worldview of many neo-pagans.[11] These need to be understood and clearly communicated to neo-pagans.

---

[7]For good treatments on this, see Mortimer J. Adler, *Truth in Religion: The Plurality of Religions and the Unity of Truth* (New York: Macmillan, 1990); Edward J. Carnell, *Introduction to Christian Apologetics* (Grand Rapids: Eerdmans, 1976), 45–62; Geisler, *Christian Apologetics*, 133–47; Geisler and Watkins, *Worlds Apart*, 105, 262–69; Nash, *Worldviews in Conflict*, 54–88.

[8]See Norman L. Geisler and Winfried Corduan, *Philosophy of Religion*, 2d ed. (Grand Rapids: Baker, 1988), 299–300; Geisler and Watkins, *Worlds Apart*, 211–16, 250–52.

[9]See Geisler, *Christian Apologetics*, 185–92; Norman L. Geisler and David K. Clark, *Apologetics in the New Age: A Christian Critique of Pantheism* (Grand Rapids: Baker, 1990), 155–221; Geisler and Watkins, *Worlds Apart*, 101–5.

[10]See Geisler, *Christian Apologetics*, 208–13; Geisler and Watkins, *Worlds Apart*, 140–45.

[11]See my book *Witchcraft: Exploring the World of Wicca* (Grand Rapids: Baker, 1996), chap. 8; Mark C. Albrecht, *Reincarnation: A Christian Critique of a New Age Doctrine* (Downers Grove, Ill.: InterVarsity Press, 1982), 51–111, 118–30; Norman L. Geisler and J. Yutaka Amano, *The Reincarnation Sensation* (Wheaton, Ill.: Tyndale, 1986), 57–86, 99–102, 107–9, 112.

II. Approaches to Avoid When Witnessing to Neo-Pagans

A. False Assumptions

1. Do not assume that they really understand all the major teachings, let alone all the nuances that their views entail.

2. Do not assume that they are conversant with what other neo-pagans practice (besides their own group). For example, do not assume that they know that some witches will hex people.

3. Do not assume one way or the other how they will respond to the gospel; just share it with them. For example, do not assume that they have committed the unpardonable sin.

4. Do not assume that they know or understand the gospel, even if they think they do. Many have major misunderstandings of Christianity.

   a. If they say they understand the gospel, then ask them politely to explain it to you, so that you can clear up any misunderstandings.

   b. If they cannot explain the gospel clearly to you, it is probably because they do not understand it.

5. Do not assume that you know the person's real motives for being involved in neo-paganism—that is, do not judge his or her motives.

B. Unhelpful Behaviors

1. Do not call neo-pagans satanists. While their views ultimately stem from the devil and fallen nature, they are technically not satanists.[12]

2. Do not think that only one approach is sufficient for every neo-pagan.

   a. Be flexible. There is no one sure-fire approach to sharing with all neo-pagans.

   b. Perhaps begin on another, related topic of mutual interest and work into sharing the gospel and the biblical perspective.

   c. The only constants are to be sensitive to and rely on the Holy Spirit, the Bible, and biblical principles; to thoughtfully consider what you say; and to have a genuine concern for the person.

3. Watch your attitude.

   a. Avoid an all-knowing attitude.

   b. Be careful about hostile body language.

   c. Avoid being argumentative.

   d. You should be respectful to neo-pagans while nonetheless strongly disagreeing with their views (1 Peter 3:15).

   e. Do not attack them, but do explain the problems with their views.

---

[12]The differences between satanism and witchcraft are clearly treated in Robert and Gretchen Passantino's book *Satanism* in this series.

    f. Try to understand—not agree with—how they see the issue(s) and why. Do not read your views onto theirs.

4. Do not just unquestioningly accept their criticisms or misunderstandings of the Bible that "everybody knows are true." Study, do your homework. Know what you believe and why.

    a. In a good sense, challenge them for evidence or examples that prove their assertions.

    b. For example, ask them to show you that the Bible is full of errors.

    c. Inform them that the God of the Bible is both transcendent and immanent. He is not immanent in the sense of being in creation, but in the sense of being active in history and in human lives and in being accessible through Jesus.

5. Don't just unquestionably accept their criticisms of Christianity.

    a. Deal with any false assumptions or stereotypes of Christianity.

    b. For example, if they should bring it up, suitably discuss charges such as the church is uncaring, everyone in it is a hypocrite, Christianity only suppresses people's freedom or creativity, Christianity is a nonparticipatory religion, and so on.

    c. If appropriate, address the false idea that Christians are only into doctrine(s) and neo-pagans are not. Explain that Christianity is a personal relationship with Jesus and that doctrines arise as we speak correctly or incorrectly about the one true God. That is, we can say true or false things about him; hence, the need for doctrine.

6. Do not get sidetracked onto tangential issues such as whether they or all neo-pagans do or believe something.

    a. Stick to the essential issues:

       (1) What are the bedrock differences between Christianity and neo-paganism?

       (2) Do people need to be saved (i.e., from their sins)?

       (3) What is necessary for salvation?

       (4) How would we know if either Christianity or neo-paganism were true?

    b. Introduce them to what is for them the unknown God (Acts 17:22–31). Introduce them to the Creator of the creation they enjoy (Acts 14:15–17), of all the beauty they admire so much. Introduce them to the "unknown God" who entered the time-space continuum to reveal himself to us. Introduce them to the gospel—to Jesus.

7. Don't let them think that Christians believe that salvation is simply attending or joining a (the) church, or being a good person or doing good things. Let them know that salvation is a personal and vital relationship with Jesus: trusting in him alone as one's Lord and Savior (John 3:16; 1 John 5:11–13).

# Part IV:
Selected Bibliography

I. Books Written by Goddess Worshipers, Witches, and Other Neo-Pagans

Adler, Margot. *Drawing Down the Moon: Witches, Druids, Goddess-Worshippers, and Other Pagans in America Today.* Revised and expanded edition. Boston: Beacon Press, 1986.

Written from the neo-pagan perspective by a witch, the definitive introduction to goddess worship, neo-paganism, and witchcraft in America.

Bonewits, Philip Emmons Isaac. *Real Magic.* Revised edition. York Beach, Maine: Samuel Weiser, 1989.

Written by a druid and materialist, the most in-depth and theoretical work on the practice and theory of magic by a neo-pagan.

Buckland, Raymond. *Buckland's Complete Book of Witchcraft.* St. Paul: Llewellyn, 1988.

A witchcraft workbook as well as a general introduction to the views and practices of contemporary witches, from one of the original popularizers of witchcraft in America, founder of Seax-Wica, and currently well-known spokesperson in the witchcraft world.

————. *Witchcraft from the Inside.* St. Paul: Llewellyn, 1971.

Budapest, Zsuzsanna Emese. *The Feminist Book of Lights and Shadows.* Venice, Calif.: Luna, 1976.

A book of shadows for Dianic—the for-women-only type of witchcraft.

Cabot, Laurie, and Tom Cowan. *Power of the Witch.* New York: Dell, 1989.

Cabot's views on the history and essential ideas and occultic practices of witchcraft, including a section on how to introduce one's children to the occult and witchcraft.

Clifton, Chas S., ed. *Witchcraft Today, Book One: The Modern Craft Movement.* St. Paul: Llewellyn, 1992.

Numerous issues relevant to the views and practices of contemporary witches, contributed by a number of leading witches.

Crowley, Vivianne. *Wicca: The Old Religion in the New Age.* San Francisco: The Aquarian Press, 1989.

Written by a high priestess in both Gardnerian and Alexandrian witchcraft, and covering many topics in contemporary witchcraft.

Crowther, Arnold, and Patricia Crowther. *The Secrets of Ancient Witchcraft with the Witches Tarot*. Secaucus, N.J.: University Books, 1974.

A general book on witchcraft from the Gardnerian perspective by friends and protégés of Gerald Gardner, with a chapter on tarot cards and a concluding section in a question-and-answer format.

_____. *The Witches Speak*. New York: Samuel Weiser, 1976.

Cunningham, Scott. *The Truth About Witchcraft Today*. St. Paul: Llewellyn, 1988.

A book on what Cunningham terms "folk magic" and witchcraft, which—though the author downplays or is naive or simply uninformed about some practices and their extent—is nonetheless a plain account of some forms of contemporary witchcraft.

Dunwich, Gernia. *Wicca Craft: The Modern Witch's Book of Herbs, Magick, and Dreams*. New York: Citadel Press, 1991.

Farrar, Stewart. *What Witches Do: The Modern Coven Revealed*. London: Sphere Books, 1973.

The views of the late Alex Sanders and Alexandrian witchcraft, based on the author's interviews and interaction with Sanders.

Farrar, Janet, and Stewart Farrar. *A Witches Bible Compleat*. New York: Magickal Childe, 1984.

A large work—formerly two books—from two leading spokespersons from the Alexandrian tradition and containing detailed information about witchcraft, rites, spells, views, and its modern history (e.g., regarding Gerald Gardner).

Frost, Gavin, and Yvonne Frost. *The Magic Power of Witchcraft*. West Nyack, N.Y.: Parker, 1976.

A presentation of some atypical views of witchcraft and the larger neo-pagan movement—e.g., their deemphasis of the Goddess, seeing witchcraft as a monotheistic religion, and their claim that they are not pagans because they do not worship nature or any named deities.

_____. *The Witches' Bible*. Reprint. New York: Berkeley, 1972.

Gardner, Gerald B. *Witchcraft Today*. London: Ride & Co., 1954.

The author's first public nonfiction work on witchcraft that unveiled his new goddess worship, which he claimed was the ancient universal pagan goddess religion, the remnants of which had survived through history.

_____. *The Meaning of Witchcraft*. London: The Aquarian Press, 1959.

A further development and unveiling of Gardner's brand of goddess worship religion.

Green, Marian. *A Witch Alone*. London: The Aquarian Press, 1991.

Jones, Prudence, and Caitlín Matthews, eds. *Voices from the Circle: The Heritage of Western Paganism*. Wellingborough, Northamptonshire, England: The Aquarian Press, 1990.

Presentations on a number of perspectives in neo-paganism—such as druidism, shamanism, and witchcraft—by major spokespersons in Europe.

Judith, Anodea. *The Truth About Neo-Paganism*. St. Paul: Llewellyn, 1994.

A concise overview of the views and practices of neo-pagans by a witch and the former president of the Church of All Worlds.

Kelly, Aidan. *Crafting the Art of Magic, Book I: A History of Modern Witchcraft, 1939–1964*. St. Paul: Llewellyn, 1991.

A reconstruction of Gerald Gardner's role in the history of early modern witchcraft, by a leading thinker in the neo-pagan movement.

Kelly, Aidan, ed. J. Gordon Melton, gen. ed. *Cults and New Religions: Neo-Pagan Witchcraft I*. New York: Garland, 1990

Leek, Sybil. *The Complete Art of Witchcraft*. New York: Signet Books, 1971.

A well-known work on witchcraft views and practices from the perspective of what some witches like to call the hereditary tradition, written by a leader in the early modern era of witchcraft.

_____. *Diary of a Witch*. New York: Signet Books, 1969.

_____. *Reincarnation: The Second Chance*. New York: Bantam Books, 1975.

Martello, Leo. *Witchcraft: The Old Religion*. Secaucus, N.J.: Citadel Press, 1973.

Roberts, Susan. *Witches, U.S.A*. New York: Dell, 1971.

Serith, Ceisiwr. *The Pagan Family: Handing the Old Ways Down*. St. Paul: Llewellyn, 1994.

Sheba, Lady (Jessica Wicker Bell). *The Book of Shadows*. St. Paul: Llewellyn, 1971.

Starhawk (Miriam Simos). *Dreaming the Dark: Magic, Sex and Politics*. New ed. Boston: Beacon Press, 1988.

_____. *The Spiral Dance: A Rebirth of the Ancient Religion of the Great Goddess*. San Francisco: Harper & Row, 1979.

Probably the best known work on witchcraft, written from a feminist position (although her rituals include men) and the Faery tradition of witchcraft.

_____. *Truth or Dare: Encounters with Power, Authority, and Magic*. San Francisco: Harper & Row, 1987.

Valiente, Doreen. *An ABC of Witchcraft: Past and Present*. New York: St. Martin's Press, 1973.

An encyclopedia of witchcraft and related concerns, views, and practices, from a woman who was instrumental in the development of Gardnerian witchcraft (e.g., she wrote "The Charge of the Goddess") and who has probably had the most influence of any witch on modern witchcraft.

————. *Natural Magic*. Reprint. Custer, Wash.: Phoenix, 1991.

————. *Where Witchcraft Lives*. London: The Aquarian Press, 1962.

————. *Witchcraft for Tomorrow*. Reprint. Custer, Wash.: Phoenix, 1987.

Weinstein, Marion. *Earth Magic: A Dianic Book of Shadows*. Revised and expanded edition. Custer, Wash.: Phoenix, 1986.

————. *Positive Magic: Occult Self-Help*. Rev. ed. Custer, Wash.: Phoenix, 1981.

Many topics relative to witchcraft and other occultic views and practices—e.g., divination, karma, reincarnation, magic, and spiritism.

Zell, Otter or Oberon (Tim), and Morning Glory Zell. *The Neo-Pagan Essence: Selected Paper from the Church of All Worlds*. Chicago: Eschaton, 1994.

II. Books Written About Goddess Worship, Witchcraft, and Other Neo-Pagan Movements (Sources Not Specifically Christian)

Ellwood, Robert. "The Edenic Bow." In *Religious and Spiritual Groups in Modern America*. Englewood Cliffs, N.J.: Prentice-Hall, 1973.

Glass, Justine. *Witchcraft, The Sixth Sense*. North Hollywood, Calif.: Wilshire Book Co., 1974.

Guiley, Rosemary Ellen. *The Encyclopedia of Witches and Witchcraft*. New York: Facts on File, 1989.

An A to Z encyclopedia of witchcraft and related occultic views and practices—on the whole, an accurate overview of witchcraft.

Jong, Erica. *Witches*. New York: Harry N. Abrams, 1981.

Luhrmann, T. M. *Persuasions of the Witch's Craft: Ritual Magic in Contemporary England*. Cambridge: Harvard University Press, 1989.

A sophisticated sociological (and otherwise) examination of (neo-)paganism, ritual magic, and witchcraft in contemporary England, based on her doctoral dissertation in social anthropology from Cambridge University.

Melton, J. Gordon. *Biographical Dictionary of American Cult and Sect Leaders*. New York: Garland, 1986.

————. *The Encyclopedia of American Religions*. 3d ed. Detroit: Gale Research, 1989.

A standard reference work on religious movements (e.g., Christianity, cults, the occult, world religions) in America.

————. *Encyclopedic Handbook of Cults in America*. New York: Garland, 1986.

————. *Magic, Witchcraft, and Paganism in America: A Bibliography*. New York: Garland, 1982.

Russell, Jeffrey Burton. *A History of Witchcraft: Sorcerers, Heretics and Pagans*. New York: Thames and Hudson, 1982.

A historical analysis and overview on many topics, including some ancient, medieval, modern, and contemporary forms of occultism as well as modern and contemporary witchcraft, by a well-known academician in this area of study.

III. Works About Goddess Worship, Witchcraft, and Other Neo-Pagan Movements (Christian Sources)

Books

Hawkins, Craig S. *Witchcraft: Exploring the World of Wicca*. Grand Rapids. Baker, 1996.

An overview of contemporary witchcraft followed by an in-depth evaluation of contemporay witchcraft using biblical and philosophical critiques.

Articles

Alexander, Brooks. "Witchcraft: From the Dark Ages to the New Age." *SCP Journal*. Vol. 16, no. 3. 1991.

A number of articles relative to the history and development of witchcraft, giving a solid analysis of the history and views of witchcraft by an evangelical researcher and thinker.

Hawkins, Craig S. "The Modern World of Witchcraft (Part One)." *Christian Research Journal*. Winter/Spring 1990.

An introduction to the modern and contemporary world of witchcraft.

_____. "The Modern World of Witchcraft (Part Two)." *Christian Research Journal*. Summer 1990.

A brief biblical and philosophical critique of contemporary witchcraft.

_____. "Witnessing to Witches." *Christian Research Journal*. Summer 1990.

Lentini, Alison. "Circle of Sisters: A Journey Through Elemental Feminism." *SCP Newsletter*. Vol. 11, no. 3. Fall 1985. 12–17.

Mather, George A., and Larry A. Nichols. "Witchcraft." *Dictionary of Cults, Sects, Religions and the Occult*. Grand Rapids: Zondervan, 1993.

A good introduction, overview, and critique of witchcraft.

Tapes

Alexander, Brooks, and Donald Frew. *Christian/Pagan Forum*. Berkeley, Calif.: Spiritual Counterfeits Project. 1986. Audio Cassette A 010. October 19.

An informative dialogue between a Christian researcher and thinker and a leading spokesperson for witchcraft (from the Covenant of the Goddess) on various aspects of and differences between Christianity and witchcraft.

Part V:
Parallel Comparison Chart

Neo-Pagans	The Bible

Revelation

Starhawk, for example, disdains what she calls the idea of "great men" who have the "one truth" to give to the "select few" because "it supports the illusion that truth is found outside, not within, and denies the authority of experience, the truth of the senses and the body, the truth that belongs to everyone and is different for everyone" (Starhawk, *Dreaming*, 22).

"In witchcraft, each of us must reveal our own truth" (Starhawk, *Spiral Dance*, 9).

"*Belief* has never seemed very relevant to the experiences and processes of the groups that call themselves, collectively, the Neo-Pagan movement" (Adler, *Drawing Down the Moon,* 20).

"What little we know of the Mysteries seems to indicate that these rites emphasized (as the Craft, at its best, does today) *experience* as opposed to *dogma*, and *metaphor* and *myth* as opposed to doctrine.... Neither emphasizes theology, belief, or the written word" (Adler, *Drawing Down the Moon,* 441, emphasis in original).

"Since Paganism allows for individual expression and mythological preference, there will perhaps never be a set of codified traditions" (Jones and Matthews, *Voices from the Circle,* 32).

"The secret things belong to the LORD our God, but the things revealed belong to us and to our children forever, that we may follow all the words of this law" (Deut. 29:29).

"All Scripture is God-breathed and is useful for teaching, rebuking, correcting and training in righteousness, so that the man of God may be thoroughly equipped for every good work" (2 Tim. 3:16).

"In the past God spoke to our forefathers through the prophets at many times and in various ways, but in these last days he has spoken to us by his Son" (Heb. 1:1–2).

God

While neo-pagans differ in their views of God, the following are representative: "[Neo-]Pagans recognize the divinity of Nature and of all living things" (Jones and Matthews, *Voices from the Circle*, 40).

"The followers of Wicca might well be considered 'duotheists'" (Adler, *Drawing Down the Moon*, 35).

"Divinity is immanent in all Nature" (Adler, *Drawing Down the Moon*, ix).

"All things in the universe are manifestations of Divinity, and as such are held to be sacred and venerable. The Gods are both immanent beings and parts of a transcendent whole" (Paul Suliin).

"It [witchcraft] is monotheistic because it is based on an underlying belief in One Life Force, One Power overall, One Essence or One Energy Source of the Universe. But witchcraft also qualifies as pagan because it acknowledges two primary aspects of deity: feminine and masculine, the Goddess and the God" (Weinstein, *Positive Magic*, 68).

"You were shown these things so that you might know that the LORD is God; besides him there is no other" (Deut. 4:35).

"Acknowledge and take to heart this day that the LORD is God in heaven above and on the earth below. There is no other" (Deut. 4:39).

"I am God, and there is no other; I am God, and there is none like me" (Isa. 46:9).

"For I am God, and not man—the Holy One among you" (Hos. 11:9b).

"They exchanged the truth of God for a lie, and worshiped and served created things rather than the Creator—who is forever praised. Amen" (Rom. 1:25).

"To the only God our Savior be glory, majesty, power and authority, through Jesus Christ our Lord, before all ages, now and forevermore! Amen" (Jude 25).

Jesus Christ

There are various views among neo-pagans regarding Jesus Christ. The following are a sample:

"I have heard of one witch who put a portrait of Jesus in her private sanctuary because, she said, he was a great white witch and knew the secret of the coven of thirteen" (Valiente, *ABC of Witchcraft*, 14).

"In the beginning was the Word, and the Word was with God, and the Word was God" (John 1:1; cf. vv. 14, 18).

"'I told you that you would die in your sins; if you do not believe that I am the one I claim to be, you will indeed die in your sins'" (John 8:24).

"I [Jesus] am the way and the truth and the life. No one comes to the Father except through me" (John 14:6).

Jesus Christ cont.

"I believe he [Jesus] was a witch. He worked miracles or what we would call magic, cured people and did most things expected from a witch. He had his coven of thirteen" (Crowther and Crowther, *Secrets of Ancient Witchcraft*, 164).

"[We reject] the Christians' insistence that Jesus was God Incarnate; that the carpenter of Nazareth . . . was in fact the creator of the Cosmos. . . . we cannot find that he ever claimed to be God. The claim seems to us to have been imposed on him later, and to be a distortion of his actual message (with which any witch or occultist would agree) that divinity resides in all of us. If it shone through him more brightly than through most other people in history, that is another matter" (Farrar and Farrar, *Witches Bible Compleat*, 2:177).

"Thomas said to him [Jesus], 'My Lord and my God!'" (John 20:28).

"Theirs are the patriarchs [the Jews], and from them is traced the human ancestry of Christ, who is God over all, forever praised! Amen" (Rom. 9:5).

"Your attitude should be the same as that of Christ Jesus: Who, being in very nature God, did not consider equality with God something to be grasped" (Phil. 2:5–6).

"Jesus said to them, 'I have shown you many great miracles from the Father. For which of these do you stone me?' 'We are not stoning you for any of these,' replied the Jews, 'but for blasphemy, because you, a mere man, claim to be god'" (John 10:32–33).

"To those who through the righteousness of our God and Savior Jesus Christ have received a faith as precious as ours" (2 Peter 1:1).

Humanity

"A spiritual path that is not stagnant ultimately leads one to the understanding of one's own divine nature. Thou art Goddess. Thou art God" (Adler, *Drawing Down the Moon*, ix).

"No matter how diverse Neo-Pagans' ideas about deities, almost all of them have some kind of 'Thou Art God/dess' concept" (Adler, *Drawing Down the Moon*, 202).

"So God created man in his own image, in the image of God he created him; male and female he created them" (Gen. 1:27).

"God is not a man, that he should lie, nor a son of man, that he should change his mind" (Num. 23:19).

"But the Egyptians are men and not God" (Isa. 31:3).

Sin

"We are aware of our own goodness and strength, and we are not afraid to admit it. We are not sinners and we know it" (Valerie Voigt, "Being a Pagan in a 9-to–5 World," 173).

"We have no concept of sin, no score card, in the way Christians understand. We have no concept of salvation, although it's certainly possible to do something wrong" (Paul Suliin, correspondence with author).

"'... for there is no one who does not sin'" (2 Chron. 6:36).

"Surely I was sinful at birth, sinful from the time my mother conceived me" (Ps. 51:5).

"All of us have become like one who is unclean, and all our righteous acts are like filthy rags" (Isa. 64:6).

"'There is no one righteous, not even one'" (Rom. 3:10).

"For all have sinned and fall short of the glory of God" (Rom. 3:23).

Reincarnation

"Most witches do believe in some form of reincarnation" (Starhawk, *Spiral Dance*, 84).

"Rebirth is not considered to be condemnation to an endless, dreary round of suffering, as in Eastern religions. Instead, it is seen as the great gift of the Goddess" (Starhawk, *Spiral Dance*, 27).

"Most Witches believe that human beings do not necessarily have immortal souls. The Craft promises 'rebirth among those you love' as the reward of the true initiates (the complete opposite of Eastern concepts)" (Kelly, *Neo-Pagan Witchcraft I*, introduction).

"There are two theories of how the circumstances of rebirth are determined. One is that the soul itself decides, based on what it feels it most needs to continue its advancement towards godhood" (Serith, *Pagan Family*, 198).

"But when the kindness and love of God our Savior appeared, he saved us, not because of righteous things we had done, but because of his mercy" (Titus 3:4–5).

"But now he has appeared once for all at the end of the ages to do away with sin by the sacrifice of himself. Just as man is destined to die once, and after that to face judgment, so Christ was sacrificed once to take away the sins of many people" (Heb. 9:26–28).

"The Lord knows how to rescue godly men from trials and to hold the unrighteous for the day of judgment, while continuing their punishment" (2 Peter 2:9).

"We are confident, I say, and would prefer to be away from the body and at home with the Lord" (2 Cor. 5:8).

Salvation

"We don't have a Devil to blame our mistakes on and we need no Savior to save us from a non-existent Hell" (Valerie Voigt, "Being a Pagan in a 9-to–5 World," 173).

"We can open new eyes and see that there is nothing to be saved *from*, no struggle of life *against* the universe, no God outside the world to be feared and obeyed" (Starhawk, *Spiral Dance*, 14).

"The kingdom of God is within you" (Adler, *Drawing Down the Moon,* 454).

"They [witches] feel that all should be free to choose the religion that best suits them. It would seem obvious that there can be no one religion for all" (Buckland, *Complete Book of Witchcraft,* 99).

"All religions lead in the same direction, simply taking different paths to get there" (Buckland, *Complete Book of Witchcraft*, 99).

"But when the kindness and love of God our Savior appeared, he saved us, not because of righteous things we had done, but because of his mercy" (Titus 3:4).

"For God so loved the world that he gave his one and only Son, that whoever believes in him shall not perish but have eternal life" (John 3:16).

"'I told you that you would die in your sins; if you do not believe that I am the one I claim to be, you will indeed die in your sins'" (John 8:24).

"Salvation is found in no one else, for there is no other name under heaven given to men by which we must be saved" (Acts 4:12).

"For the wages of sin is death, but the gift of God is eternal life in Christ Jesus our Lord" (Rom. 6:23).

"If you confess with your mouth, 'Jesus is Lord,' and believe in your heart that God raised him from the dead, you will be saved" (Rom. 10:9).

"For it is by grace you have been saved, through faith—and this not from yourselves, it is the gift of God—not by works, so that no one can boast" (Eph. 2:8–9).

Occultic Practices

"In Wicca it's [magic] given a more prominent place.... Wicca is a religion that embraces magic" (Cunningham, *Truth About Witchcraft*, 64–65).

"Wicca is magic" (Stewart Farrar, *What Witches Do*, 137).

"Magic ... is an element common to all traditions of Witchcraft" and "Magic is the craft of Witchcraft" (Starhawk, *Spiral Dance*, 13, 109).

"One of the objects of present-day witches' rites is to contact the spirits of those who have been witches in their past lives on earth" (Valiente, *ABC of Witchcraft*, 157).

"I always encourage children to have dreams ... in which they will meet their spirit guides or animal helpers" (Cabot, in Cabot and Cowan, *Power of the Witch*, 278).

"Divination in all its forms has always been an important part of the witch's craft" (Valiente, *ABC of Witchcraft*, 117).

"Let no one be found among you ... who practices divination or sorcery, interprets omens, engages in witchcraft, or casts spells, or who is a medium or spiritist or who consults the dead. Anyone who does these things is detestable to the LORD" (Deut. 18:10–12).

"I warn you, as I did before, that those who live like this [e.g., including those who practice witchcraft—v. 20] will not inherit the kingdom of God" (Gal. 5:21).

"Nor did they repent of their murders, their magic arts, their sexual immorality or their thefts" (Rev. 9:21).

"'But the cowardly, the unbelieving, the vile, the murderers, the sexually immoral, those who practice magic arts, the idolaters and all liars—their place will be in the fiery lake of burning sulfur. This is the second death'" (Rev. 21:8).

Part VI:
Glossary

Adept   Someone who is proficient in or a master of occultic matters.

Book of   A witch's personal or customized grimoire. Books of shadows may
shadows   belong to individual witches or to a coven collectively. Although
                       they vary significantly in content, they often serve as spiritual
                       diaries or journals, commonly containing the witches' experi-
                       ences and experiments, along with reflections on matters rele-
                       vant to their tradition and practice of witchcraft. They also often
                       function as personal handbooks or textbooks.

Coven   The basic social unit of witches who regularly meet in groups
                       (sometimes referred to as groves, circles, or nests—terms more
                       commonly used among nonwitch neo-pagans). A coven typically
                       has anywhere from three to thirty members, but thirteen is the
                       ideal. Most covens admit both males and females and often seek a
                       balanced representation of the two genders. Covens that admit
                       only females are one type of Dianic (feminist) coven and consider
                       themselves a *womins* or *wimin's* religion or spirituality movement.
                       There are relatively few exclusively male (e.g., homosexual) covens.

Craft or   The name a witch or other neo-pagan chooses for oneself upon
magical name   initiation into witchcraft or other forms of neo-paganism. For ex-
                       ample, Miriam Simos's craft name is Starhawk.

Divination   The attempt to obtain information regarding the past, present, or
                       future by occultic means. Forms of divination include altered
                       states of consciousness (e.g., channeling or other trance states), as-
                       trology, crystal gazing, *I Ching,* mediumship, numerology, palm-
                       istry, runes, scrying, and taort cards among others.

Goddess   The worshiping or invoking or experiencing of the Goddess (or
worship   goddesses), however she (or they) is conceived of by the worshiper.

Grimoires   Ancient, modern, or contemporary magical texts, such as the
                       witches' book of shadows or *The Greater Key of Solomon the King.*
                       They generally contain instructions for casting spells and other
                       forms of working magic, practicing divination, and spiritism.

Magic/sorcery   The attempt to cause changes to occur in conformity with one's will through occultic methods. It is the supposed ability to bend, control, direct, influence, manipulate, or otherwise turn reality for one's objectives, allegedly accomplished by invoking or utilizing mysterious or invisible forces, spirits, or other extradimensional entities or beings, or relatively unknown forces, laws, powers, or rules to manipulate reality. *Magic* in the sense used means *sorcery* and is not to be confused with prestidigitation or sleight-of-hand.

Necromancy   The attempt to communicate with, contact, or summon the spirits of the dead. It is one form of spiritism and can be a form of divination or magic/sorcery.

Neo-paganism   The new paganism—a nature-oriented religious movement whose followers either are nature worshipers or have a very high regard for nature. It includes the reinventing or revival of the old gods and goddesses of pre-Christian polytheistic mythologies, mystery cults, and nature religions, such as Celtic, Greek, Egyptian, Roman, or Sumerian, or the interest in existing tribal religions (e.g., Native American religions) and shamanism, or the making of new religions (see Part I, Section I.A.3.a–e).

Solitary Practitioners   Some witches practice witchcraft independent of or separate from a coven. They are generally referred to as solitary practitioners.

Spiritism   Contact, interaction, or trafficking with noncorporeal entities.

Summerland   For many neo-pagans, the place where one's soul or immaterial nature goes temporarily after death and where it is said to rest and be refreshed and made ready for reincarnation into another body. It or its counterparts are also referred to by many other names such as the Otherworld, the Land of Faerie, or Tir na nOg.

Wiccans   Witches, practitioners of witchcraft.

Witch   A term applied to both males and to females who practice witchcraft. Contrary to popular opinion, male witches are not called warlocks in witchcraft.

Witchcraft   A generic term representing only the various perspectives or traditions of contemporary neo-pagan witchcraft, which is also referred to as "the Old Religion," "the craft," "the craft of the wise," and "Wicca." Witchcraft is a nature-oriented religion whose followers are polytheists and/or pantheists and/or panenthesists. While they may have a number of deities, generally the primary ones are the Mother Goddess and the Horned God.

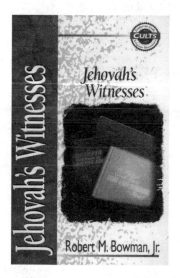

We want to hear from you. Please send your comments about this book
to us in care of the address below. Thank you.

ZondervanPublishingHouse
Grand Rapids, Michigan 49530
http://www.zondervan.com